A New View of Modern History

Book 7 History of Mankind

By Steve Preston

3rd Edition
2018

Table of Contents

Introduction

This book covers what you would think was "normal history" up until the 20th century. It covers the last three thousand years and, as we have seen, what is taught and what the evidence shows are very different. During that time there have been some pretty amazing things happen that you probably not told as our histories are systematically changed until very little truth remains. Some of the events are not very flattering to our "heroes", so it was decided not to teach our children about them. The evidence shows the following:

- **Columbus was not looking for China** and he brought back syphilis when he couldn't find gold.

- **UFOs were seen** in abundance in the Middle Ages and there is proof. Artists drew the images that people take pictures of today.

- **The pilots of these "air" crafts** were not only seen by crazies and depictions of a similar pilots have been found around the world. The proof is astounding.

- **Moslems invented Germ Warfare** and used it effectively over a thousand years ago.

- **Romans took over Britain but most don't know why.** They needed it so badly---[The answer, most likely, was copper and the story is not typically told].

- **Romans didn't bath** in their communal bathhouses. They scraped. This scraping caught on around the world. Soon everyone was scraping his body clean.

- **The Pilgrims** were grave robbing pirates. I know you were told a different "cleaned up" version of the story.

- **The Puritans** were slave traders, so it is beyond me why they are called Puritans.

- **The first U.S. President was not Washington**; in fact, Washington didn't take over until 1789 some 24 years after our first Declaration of Independence and 13 years after the second one as we were governed by 15 Presidents.

- **A Submarine** and helped win the Revolutionary War.

- **Manifest Destiny** was a farce

- **Five Civil Wars** have been fought so far and a 6th one almost started.

- **New Hampshire** caused the 5th Civil War, not slavery.

- **35 thousand slave owners** were protected during the 1861 Civil War.

- **The first and 2nd slave Presidents** in USA were not black.

- **The Industrial Revolution and Manifest Destiny** were ploys to force Fascism and make ¾ of the richest Americans, prior to 2008, wealthy beyond belief while the rest of the country suffered 3 great depressions. It was initiated by the Civil War and it almost destroyed the United States.

- **Congress passed the 13th Amendment** that insured that slavery was a State issue only

- **The Emancipation Proclamation** didn't free the slaves.

- **The 13th, 14th, & 15th Amendments** to the Constitution are illegal.

For some reason you keep reading these books and from the previous six books, you must be aware by now that you have been lied to by scientists, governments, historians, and religious dogma. As with the other books, we will move outside the box and look at more of the evidence around you so that a better understanding of the "Absolute Truth" can be possible. This book is different in that the timeline of history is generally known and I will not be trying to repeat well-known elements. Instead I will be picking out some specific elements of our history to expand what we think we know. By cross-comparison of information from around the world; from examination of different religious records; and from looking at generally disregarded scientific research; this history will, hopefully, bring you an enlightened picture.

Two Mistakes-I've always been told there are two mistakes that a historian can make. He can either ignore all evidence he doesn't like or he can accept all apparent evidence as a matter of fact. Of the two, I believe the first is the worst, as it gives absolutely no hope at gaining truth. The second may not lead to the truth, but there is at least some chance in its attainment.

Evolution-Some may tell you that presenting ideas that only tell part of the truth is bad. In fact, throughout much of my writings, I have implied that very thing, but it is not a reasonable belief nor is it the belief of this writer. What I have been trying to impress on readers is that holding on to a truth even after it has to be verified by stating that some elements are "anomalous" or "simply don't fit in the model" is dangerous. If we take Darwin's evolution; his theory was great. After the anomalies started showing up; those anomalies should have been identified and used to expand our awareness rather than simply ignoring items that didn't fit.

The same should be done with ALL studies. In this book, I will provide the ANOMALIES to be mixed in with what you "Think" you know about this era. You can disregard the information or use it. Either way, you will have expanded your awareness of this time period. If you have read the first creation books you are very aware of the ancient recollection of the time before the flood. If you haven't, or just as a matter of review, here is a quick overview to bring you up to beginning of this book.

Book One & Two

In the first two books we found out that there were two creations of mankind before Adam. We also investigated some physical observations of our earth as well those on other planets. We found out that huge destruction periods, death, life on other planets, and many things were described in these ancient texts, but the details were not in abundance, especially for the very ancient humans that inhabited the planets. Some of the details may have seemed fanciful, but the information, none-the-less, it was provided to us by ancient writers and examination of physical evidence. I simply brought the information together so that the details were more readily understood. The timeline of these events was not designed around external pressure for consistency, but rather used the consistency obtained from cross comparison of ancient data and artifacts. Here are some of the elements that were discovered. Originally, the consistency and orbits of the various planets was, shall we say, questionable. As the planets changed their sizes and densities, they moved to different positions and sometimes they even got close enough to affect one another. Mars and Earth probably had several "close encounters" which helped form their surfaces and helped reposition them into their current orbits.

Pre Adam Humans-Ancient records indicated that beings we call angels coexisted with or came from a being that looked almost exactly like us. I called this being " the ancient human".

6th Day Man-The second book discussed a second creation of humans that were not as evolved as the ancient humans. I called this group of humans the 6th day man in reference to the description provided in the Old Testament of the Bible. A group of angels that had been kicked out of heaven came to force the evolution of these new humans. The ancient Jewish people called these "bad" angels the Nephilim.

8

The Hybrid Race- These Nephilim went so far as inbreeding with the primitive man. What a difference! The ancient texts said the hair all over their bodies seemed to go away overnight. They became very smart, but now they were too smart to do the bidding nor worship the Nephilim. The lazy Nephilim believed that this new "hybrid race" was practically useless. The Nephilim still had to work and take care of the tree-of-life that was used to keep them young and they begged God for more help and that is where book three came in.

Book 3 & 4

God came to the rescue about 40 thousand years ago. The third and 4th books talked about the time from the creation of the third man, called Adam, up until the destruction of the world by Flood. Here are some of the highlights. We only had 40 thousand years to talk about in the 2 books.

The Third Adam- God made a better man and the Bible called him Adam. This time, God made man differently. He made man with the very thing taken away from the angels that had been kicked out of heaven. The ancient texts simply called it "the light". The Nephilim wanted "the light" back. They thought that one way to regain the "light" was to breed with Adam and Eve.

Adam, Eve and Sex- The ancient texts said that Eve, the first Adamic woman, and Adam, the first Adamic man, both went against the wishes of God and probably had sex with the Nephilim and things really started to happen bad for the Adamic humans. They were kicked out of the Garden of Eden; they started wearing clothes; and they had children. Some of the children were "mixed breeds", because of Nephilimic sex. I called the offspring of Adamics and Nephilim the "Adamic hybrids" to sort of keep them segregated from the other half dozen type of humans. According to ancient texts, this "hybrid" race still had a problem with the "light" thing I mentioned before. The problem will get fixed in this book, but from the time of Adam until 2

9

thousand years ago only the "Pure Adamics" were considered to be God's "Chosen People".

*Nephadim-*Very soon after Adam was kicked out of Eden, we read about a new type of human that created more problems. This new human was originally one of 200 angels that wanted to experience human things. This "humanized spirit creature" was called the Nephadim according to ancient Jewish texts. The new human had children with the other various humans and it was just a mess.

*War-*It got even worse when wars erupted. I'm talking about nuclear, worldwide and even planetary wars with all the science fiction type things like flying saucers. Even lightning weapons of some sort were invented and evidently used. The scars and evidence of this terrible time in history are still extant, but it still got worse.

*Meteors and Comets-*Stones from the sky fell on many parts of the preflood world. The meteors destroyed many populations. Then the Earth shifted its rotational axis, which didn't sit too well with the inhabitants. Mighty earthquakes cracked open the earth. Major island civilizations, like the famed Atlantis, sank into the seas. By the time of the shift in the earth's rotation an Adamic man named Noah had come along. There were thousands and thousands of Adamic hybrids and only a few pureblood Adamic humans living on the earth. A new beginning came when the entire world was flooded. A year later, Noah and his family, who had been living in a boat, came to dry land; got out of their boat; saw a rainbow; began growing grapes; and worshiped God. This flood generally ended the world and the 4th book.

Books 5 & 6

*A Babel Tower -*Most remember the story as the Tower of Babel incident, but we found out, in book 5, that the incident was also remembered around the world. We also found out that not everything was lost during the flood. Much of the ancient knowledge survived. While many choose not to believe it, we discovered that Noah's family was not the only family to survive the flood.

As we went a few thousand years in the future, we came to a human called Nimrod. He and a few hundred thousand of his friends built the huge Tower of Babel as some type of launching platform to begin an assault on heaven. God, of course, didn't like that and destroyed the tower. Something happened when all this was taking place and the human brain began to atrophy.

Brain Atrophy-Of course, the brain is not the only thing that has atrophied over time. The picture below shows how lack of use of organs causes them to reduce in size just like our brain. This also shows that the loss of use of our immense brain happened fairly recently because the brain size has not shrunken substantially. Our third eyelid, appendix, and ear point have all but gone and a whale's legs are just about useless, while our brain is still pretty good, because the atrophy thing happened only about 5 thousand years ago.

War & Darkness-Even with our brain defects, humans loved to kill each other and a war broke out some time during or after the Tower incident. It was a doosy. To make thing worse, about this same time the earth was plunged into the first of 4, fairly recent, Dark Ages. Some more time passed and a second Dark Age occurred which forced the Adamic tribes to go to Egypt. They stayed there for a while, and there were some plagues, so Moses and the Adamic/Jews left. They wandered and herded for about 400 years while Assyrians, Babylonians, and Egyptians jockeyed for control.

Greek Dark Age-A third major Dark Age occurred and the outcome was the end of the Nephilim and their gigantic, direct descendants. The Jews became a major ruling group in the Middle East and that puts us up to this book.

This Book

This is a run of the mill history with a twist. It starts about 3 thousand years ago. People are just now coming out of a terrible Dark Age similar to that of the Middle Ages. We will find out in this book that flying ships were still around and pilots looked a little strange. We will also discuss more about levitation, re-discovering America, incorrect histories, and many more subjects. These are all aimed at showing you that relying on what you have been told about history is dangerous. There are too many people with agendas that want you to believe things that have little to do with the truth. Those who try to provide unbiased histories also mess up the truth because they wish to make the reader comfortable. As I have stated before, this is not a comfortable history.

Misinformation-We will discuss many misdirected histories that were initiated, believed, and used as the basis for our knowledge of our past. We will find out that that misinformation follows all the way to our present day by looking at various commonly known stories and the fallacies that are apparent.

Information Sources-There are a limited number of footnoted elements and direct access information trails in this book. While that make the information more concise, I'm sure some will find it more uncomfortable and will not have as much faith in the details. When the information comes from ancient texts, I usually provide the ancient verse and provide more details about the texts in the back of the book. When the information comes from archeological discoveries, I have not always provided sources, but I have provided an annotated Bibliography, which will most likely lead you to the roots of the information and there is always the internet. All I can say is that the information was not made up by me. That is not to say that some of the data could have been contrived or misinterpreted by others and it certainly doesn't mean that I have not misinterpreted details, so all you will finally have is a timeline and data that should start you on a path of truth.

Historical Theorists-As I stated many times now, it would be impossible to acknowledge all of the researchers that have been responsible for bringing to the surface all of the ideas that connect to produce this historical record. I have tried to identify key people where I could remember details and if I have left out key researchers it was not intentional. The great researchers like Robert Bauval, Graham Hancock, Christopher Dunn, Richard Hoagland, Charles Hapsgood, Anthony West, David Hatcher Childress, Lewis Spence, Richard Noone, Rand and Rose Flemath, Herbie Brennan, Charles Berlitz, Zecharia Sitchin, Erich Von Daniken, and many others have opened our eyes to a much broader sense of reality and deserve our gratitude. Some of the research is indicated in the Bibliography section at the end of the book.

Controversy

Controversy in Science- The list below shows some of the somewhat controversial scientific topics that will be discussed in this book. Please check your opinion before and after reading this history.

- Spontaneous Human combustion is real
- Columbus brought Syphilis to Europe
- Bell didn't invent the telephone
- Franklin didn't invent the Franklin stove
- Marconi didn't invent the Radio
- Flying saucers survived the Tower of Babel incident.
- A Submarine was used in the Revolutionary War

Controversy in Religion- The list below shows some of the somewhat controversial religious topics that will be discussed.

- There has been a fifth creation of man
- Jesus Christ was real and was the incarnation of God
- The thing taken from the rebel angels some 500 thousand years earlier was brought back with Jesus.
- The thing Jesus brought turned humans into a new creation.

Controversy in History- The list below shows some of the somewhat controversial topics concerning History that will be discussed.

- Romans didn't bathe in their public baths
- Nero and Caligula were loved by the Roman people and the Jews. OK! Maybe not the Jews.
- Nero married a man but had him castrated first so it wouldn't look bad.
- Christopher Columbus was a liar, and a "young girl slave-trader", who wasn't looking for China.
- Someone was actually swallowed by a whale and survived.
- Hip-hip-hurray should never be said by a Moslem
- The Pilgrims were grave robbing pirates.
- The "Civil War" didn't really have anything to do with Slavery.
- New Hampshire Started the Civil War
- The Emancipation Proclamation didn't free the slaves.
- Abraham Lincoln promoted and bought Slaves
- Lincoln was the least popular person ever to be elected president
- President Jefferson eliminated Slavery
- The first slave president in USA wasn't black
- Slaves settled America
- The thirteenth U.S. President used lead teeth because he only had one tooth of his own.

- One of the US presidents only served one day.
- The first US president only served one year; in fact, the first 7 presidents had very short terms in office.

Disclaimer:

This history is not the absolute truth nor does it use the Anderson Truth Model.

This history shows elements that should be considered when trying to determine truth, but the "More commonly known truth" has been left out because most already know that one. Therefore, this portion of this history series is biased. It is not biased by a particular belief, but rather by exclusion of commonly known data.

Don't take the words in this book a gospel. In fact, don't take the words of any book as being completely true. All books have errors or incorrect assumptions. This is only one timeline that tries to show another viewpoint of our history. It is up to the reader to take away from this work that which can best aid him in establishing the truth. Speaking of timeline, the following shows what this book will cover.

Book 7 Timeline

Date	Description
1000-600BC	Babylonian, Akkadian, and Persians rule the Middle East
600-400BC	Macedonian/Greek Rule
400BC –0	Pre-Christian Rome- Conquering the world for entertainment
0-500AD	Post-Christian Rome- The new form of entertainment
500-1000AD	European Dark Ages [Meteors hit]-Age of the Moslem Expansion
1000-1200AD	Stupid Crusades and the Age of the Catholic Church
1200-1400AD	Age of Science Re-discovery
1400-1600AD	Age if American Re-re-discovery
1600-1800AD	Age of Colonization and slavery
1800-1900AD	Age of Industrialization
1900-2000AD	Atomic and Space Age
	Less than 3 thousand years

750-400BC Greek City States

With that let's get started. We've traveled through thousands of years, but there is still more discussion that is needed before we get to America's 5th Civil War, including a discussion about the last creation of mankind. Before we get to that, we might as well start with the Greeks, because everyone talks about them as if they invented ancient history. It wasn't always that way. The Greeks, initially, were quiet communities of small city-states that continually fought one another on a small scale but didn't stir the world pot. As far as heritage, they were not pure Adamics. While the Adamics stayed close to the ancient Canaanite stronghold, the Nephilim had inhabited the Greek land just like they had inhabited and ruled other lands around the world. Like almost all people of the world, the Greeks were hybrids-part Adamic and part Nephilimic. After the Nephilim had all gone, the Greeks prided themselves as being a democracy for all non-slaves, non-female citizens [Slaves and women didn't count]. They also wrote books and plays and tried to make everyone believe that the earth was flat.

Mythology

As part of these books and plays, they did something important to our understanding of the past. Many of the ancient Nephilim stories were written down in documents we call myths today. When they were written they were supposed to be a very detailed accounting of what had been passed down over thousands of years. Some of the details got muddled as they tried to put a lesson in every story. That was a major mistake because history, sometimes, has no lesson to tell. At least they tried to tell about mankind's history. A lot of it didn't make sense to them and,

17

therefore, it was presented in a fairytale way. Inside all of the fluff, there is "real" information that can help us "remember" our ancient past. Instead we scoff at gods [or angels] acting like spoiled humans and turn around and accept the fact that another angel named Satan acted just like a spoiled human and tried to take control of heaven because he was the most beautiful angel of them all. We scoff at Pegasus the flying horse, but accept Peter walking across the sea or Ezekiel seeing a 4 headed flying thing with a multitude of wings and something described as a wheel inside a wheel.

Let's see how very different the Greek Mythology really is when compared to other ancient histories and evidence. This chronology comes from Hesiod around the 8th century BC.

	Greek History	Biblical History
1.	In the very ancient times God [Cronus] human beings were eternally young	Exactly like the ancient humans examined in book 1
2.	The earth covered over this race of men	Just like the Biblical account and other ancient descriptions, a war destroys just about everything including the ancient humans
3.	The spirits of these ancient humans became guardian Spirits	Just as I had previously brought out. There is a lot of evidence that the group we call "angels" are the spirits of the ancient humans.
4.	Zeus [son of Cronus] created a new [inferior] human race. They would not worship the gods, so the gods destroyed them.	This is very similar to the race created on the 6th day. As I discussed in book 2, they became too smart.
5.	Zeus experimented on a new race of humans who became warlike and destroyed each other.	This is exactly like the ancient descriptions of the race called the Nephadim and their offspring.
6.	The race of demi-gods came next. They were half god-half human.	This is exactly the same as the Nephilim and their offspring.
7.	Zeus then created the present type human. They became terribly wicked.	Adam was created, but most of the humans during this time became evil as indicated in the Biblical references.
8.	Zeus destroyed all but 3 of these new humans by flooding the entire world.	The worldwide flood is almost identical to the Biblical account

Instead of reading about the details of the gods [our ancient half angel half man rulers] while thinking they are simply fantasies, we study the similarities of the myths with all the other similar stories that are still extant from around the world. We should also study the creativity of the Greeks in war.

Trojan War Creativity

These Greeks were great sailors for the time and established trade communities from Spain to the eastern edge of the Back Sea. None of that seems to be memorable. The thing that most people remember is one possible contact with the people of Turkey, or Troy to be exact. This contact ended in the Greek's favor. The Greeks made a horse and won a war by being sneaky rather than having the best army. That brings us to the Egyptians.

Egyptian Trojan Horse-Let's look at this wooden horse for a little. The Greeks started feeling great when they went to war with a large horse to conquer the City of Troy. I'm not going to try to determine whether the incident actually happened or didn't happen, but what I want to share is that this was not the first Trojan horse idea. The Egyptians used the same tactic around 1500BC, but they used a Mule, so the Greeks weren't as sneaky as we have all thought. They just knew when to borrow a good idea.

According to the "Papyrus Harris 500", from the reign of Thutmose III [show above right], we can read about the exploits of General Djehuty, including his legendary capture of Joppa. *This was accomplished by sending the Joppans a gift. The gift was a large quantity of basket-laden mules [see above left], but inside the baskets, Djehuty forgot to put any presents. Instead he*

put his soldiers inside the baskets. The Joppans gladly received the basket ladened donkeys, but soon they wanted to return the gift for something with less killing. All the Greeks had to do was to read the ancient manuscripts and make a bigger mule. That brings us to the Chinese.

Chinese Trojan ~~Horse~~ Virgins-By the way, later in the book we will discuss how the Chinese changed the Trojan Horse trick in a very inventive way. It seems like everyone used this tactic and everyone got fooled by it. The people of Troy brought in their present and lost the war with the Greeks just like the Joppans lost their war with the Egyptians. While the horse thing was interesting, the Greeks weren't really known for their warring capability. They were known for their Religious dominance.

Greeks Gain Religious Power

One of the signs of religious power in Greece was the Acropolis. It was a "Hill Monument" to their "gods". Hopefully you are beginning to believe that not all of the creatures in their "Mythology Stories" were imaginary, but by the time the Greeks had built the Acropolis, in 438 BC, all of the Nephilim/gods were undoubtedly dead. Their devotion to these rouge angels probably didn't help them gain favor with God, but the Acropolian site itself is spectacular and shows how strong their religion was in the region. Greeks controlled European religion so much that when the Romans took control, they used the Greek religion as their own and changed the names to make them feel better about it. I've had the privilege of investigating several of the ancient Greek sites. The picture below shows the author investigating a temple just behind the Parthenon. This temple contained the alters to Athena [Goddess of wisdom], Poseidon [God of the Sea], and Hephaestus [God of metalworking] was of special interest. It signified all that was Greece. Their metalworking and other artistry were unparalleled; they were fine seamen; and Athena was their patron goddess where wisdom was valued above most other things. It should be noted that Athena was a hybrid. She was

20

half Titan [giant] and half normal god [from Zeus]. This type of half-breed could very well have ruled Greece in the very ancient times.

Greeks Gain Scientific Power

Not only were they establishing themselves in war and religion, but also the Greeks were known for enlightenment. From the discussions so far, I think you can tell that their enlightenment was somewhat limited. They did; however, rediscover many scientific truisms. Here is one of those "enlightened" moments. On one occasion, several Greek philosophers had gathered to discuss how many teeth a woman had. Since men had thirty-two teeth, and women were ``inferior", they all had decided that the latter had fewer --- twenty-eight --- teeth. Not one of them had suggested that they might open a woman's mouth and count the teeth, so the count remained a scientific fact.

Middle East Power Struggle

732-609 Assyrian Empire

While the entire Greek City-State thing was going on and the Greeks were gaining enlightenment, the Middle East was in complete turmoil as the Jewish kingdom fell apart. The Assyrians didn't go away, they just bided their time. Under Sargon II, the Assyrians destroyed the Jewish Empire and set up shop again. Assurbanipal, his successor, did the same and expanded the empire, but what he is really known for was his library, for which we will be forever grateful. Much of what we know about the ancient Middle Eastern culture we owe to the libraries of the capitol city named Nineveh. Luckily, they were not found and destroyed like most of the other libraries around the world. The palace of Nineveh was unbreachable with 3 layers of walls around the perimeter.

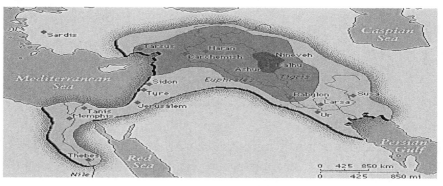

605-559 Chaldea-Babylonian Empire

Somehow the Babylonians decided that they didn't like the Assyrians again, so Nebuchadnezzer II took the Assyrian land back with more killing. They even breached the unbreachable walls of Nineveh, but the Persians didn't let the Babylonians bask in glory for long. The "Hanging Gardens" was constructed in the great city of Babylon before the Persians came and the walls to the city were built up to a height of 350 feet high. Certainly no one would bother the mighty Babylonians.

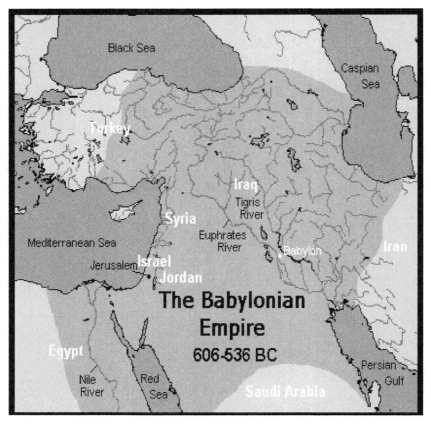

The Hanging Gardens-The Hanging Gardens is pictured in the foreground [left below], but the temple of Jupiter shown in the background was just as impressive. It was 650 feet high and ¼ mile per side at the base. King Nebuchadnezzer indicated that he **repaired** the tower, which was built by an ancient king and damaged by time and earthquakes. Many have thought that it was the tower of Babel from the past. No wonder the Persians could take them. They were not interested in fighting, just building monuments.

 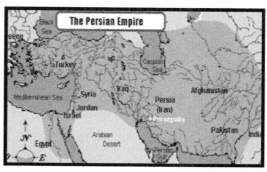

559-330BC- Persian Empire

Cyrus the Great initiated the Persian Empire, shown in the map above, and the Babylonians were out. He didn't try to breech the mighty wall, but instead, went under it and Babylonian greatness became a memory. Then Darius took over Mellitus and the Persians were off to a great start at taking over the world. Xerxes followed Darius and took over Greece with 180 thousand men. He even took over Egypt in 343BC. The Greeks then tried to take back their land in 400 BC, but it didn't end that way they wanted it to. That war is comically called the "Retreat of 10 thousand".

When it was all over, the Persian Empire had taken over more land than any other post Babel entity as shown above. Not only was the standard Middle East under their control but also Egypt and Turkey. Finally, the Macedonians changed all of the fun times for the Persians.

350-323BC-Macedonian Empire

The Persians were going down and King Philip of Macedonia started it all by killing and conquering in Greece and the Turkish area. His son, Alexander, learned from him and killed his Uncle and possibly killed his father as well. He had a knack for it, so he conquered the rest of the Middle Eastern world before he, himself, died. In one battle, Plutarch wrote that he killed 100 thousand Persians. The Persians were out of the picture, but the Alexander the "Great" thing was uncalled for unless you want to think of him as a great butcher. The picture above shows the extent of his wanderings and killing.

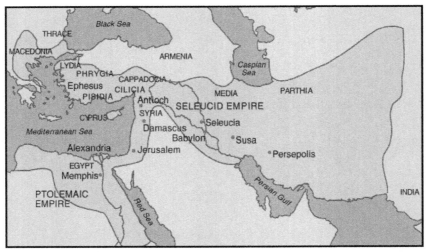

Alexander the Fake

Did Alexander the "Supposedly Great" conquer the world? Did he cry because he had no more worlds to conquer as has been said many times? Did he carry himself as an Enlightened Despot to establish the first true world government as is taught in our schools? If you said "no" to all of these, you read the more true histories rather than listening to the fables typically brought out as fact in established history books. According to Roman accounts by Curtius, Justin, Diodorus, Arrian, Plutarch and Ethiopic Texts, Alexander was defeated in India by King Porus and had to make a treaty with him to save himself and his soldiers' lives. He cried, all right, but because he was a broken man not because he needed more worlds to conquer. He started into India with 40 thousand men and left, defeated, with only 15 thousand remaining, according to modern Macedonian Age investigators like Robin Poole. As far as his having insight and compassion in his ruling methods, let's just examine some of the facts including losing, crying, and killing.

He Lost-According to many ancient texts including various Roman and Ethiopic texts, Alexander almost lost everything to the Indian King Porus. Mr. E. Badge writes the following from the Ethiopic version: "In the battle of Jhelum a large majority of Alexander's cavalry were killed. Alexander realized that if he were to continue fighting he would be completely ruined. He requested Porus to stop fighting. Porus was true to Indian traditions and did not kill the surrendered enemy. After this both signed treaty, Alexander then helped King Porus in annexing other territories to his kingdom".

He cried-Here is his cry scene. "Porus, please pardon me. I have realized your bravery and strength. Now I cannot bear these agonies. With a sad heart I am planning to put an end to my life. I do not desire that my soldiers should also be ruined like me. I am that culprit who has thrust them into the jaws of death. It does not become a king to thrust his soldiers into the jaws of death."

27

He killed-Here is a depiction of his benevolence: Basus of Bactria fought with Alexander to defend the freedom of his motherland. He was brought before Alexander as a prisoner, Alexander ordered his servants to whip him and then cut off his nose and ears. That wasn't enough fun so Alexander then killed him. He also killed Aristotle's nephew simply because Kalasthenese had criticized him for imitating the Persian emperors. He murdered his father's lieutenant for fun, most of the Persian generals, and even his friend Clytus when he got angry.

His greatness is a fraud and his name should be Alexander the Fake

330-30BC Greek Kings Ruled Egypt

As a Macedonian and before his defeat in India, Alexander conquered Egypt and put his own ruling group in charge, but the Macedonians liked Greek philosophy, so many thought of themselves as Greeks. Pretty soon there was no difference between Macedonia and Greece. The Egyptians kept their name, but they were turned into another Greece. This was a time of great learning, philosophy, and libraries that ended with Cleopatra VII. She killed herself with an asp and Egypt was turned into a Roman state after the 300-year "Greek" reign. We'll talk about Cleopatra in a little more detail below as soon as the Roman Empire is examined.

28

200BC-500AD Roman Empire

The Romans took over everything including most of Europe, northern Africa, Persia, and Egypt as shown above. For sport, the Romans had conquered people try to fight bears and lions for sport. Usually the people came in second place. Sometimes Christians and others were tied in a chair in the center of an arena and slowly would have their skin removed to the cheers of the morbid crowds. These depictions seem terrible, but the Romans weren't all bad and they brought order into a crazy world. Everything was going well for the Romans, but then they came up with a new term called Orgy. Yep, you guessed it, after that time, the Roman Empire began to collapse, because that was all they wanted to do.

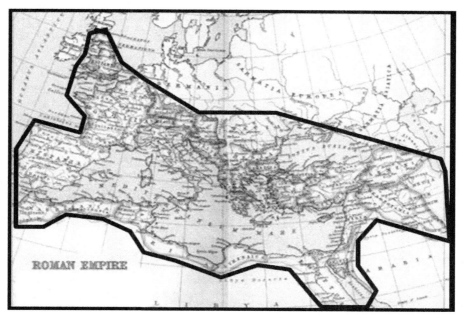

ROMAN EMPIRE

Right in the middle of the time-period that the Romans controlled much of the world there were many colorful individuals that were somewhat misunderstood. I'm selecting 5 simply because of misconceptions rather than historical necessity, however, one of these individuals is very important, as you will soon see.

The first is remembered for being nude and the second is remembered for being vengeful. The third one in the list is by far the most important as he initiated the 5th creation of mankind as he was God incarnate. The last three were thought of as bad leaders and some of their identity was unfounded. I'm talking about Cleopatra, Botadicea, Jesus, Caligula, Nero, and Commode. As you can see they are brought out in relation to time rather than importance. Cleopatra is first up.

69-30BC Cleopatra

When we talk about Cleopatra we really mean Cleopatra VII. She was not a great beauty, but she didn't wear many clothes either as shown below. Born in 69BC, she was one of the "Greeks" that took the throne of Egypt when she married her 10-year-old brother. She was unfaithful to the kid and had sex with Julius Caesar, who was the Emperor of Rome. After a couple of years of marriage, her husband started becoming interested in sex so Cleopatra had Julius kill him. Then she married an even younger brother so that she would have more "time" for her "outside" interests. Soon she got pregnant by Julius, so Julius knew what he had to do. He went home and married a Roman woman. Julius was eventually stabbed and died so Mark Antony and Octavius became part of the new three-part ruling unit of Rome. Antony decided that the portion of the empire containing Egypt should be his because he liked the way Cleopatra didn't wear clothes. In fact, Antony liked her so much, he divorced his wife, who was the sister of Octavius, and Cleopatra soon had some more Roman kids.

Octavius didn't like Antony after that and war began. Within a couple of years, it was over. Mark Antony and Cleopatra committed suicide. Octavius made sure that the Roman kids were all killed as well and Egypt became part of the Roman Empire. A few other things happened, but that is a quick overview.

Beetle Beauty-One reason Cleopatra was so attractive was her glittering eyes. She smeared crushed beetle shells on her eyelids almost every day to impress her suitors. Now that is an important piece of history don't you think?

Cleopatras- Cleopatra VII was a plain looking queen that didn't wear clothes. Her two Greek husbands ages 10 and 9 both died and she still was able to have children by Julius Caesar and Mark Antony. While this particular Cleopatra is somewhat discussed in history textbooks. The whole lot of Cleopatras were just about like number 7. Here are a few examples as most intermarried so much, it's no wonder they kept forgetting to wear clothing.

Cleopatras	Ruled [BC]	Description
Cleo-I	193-176	Married Ptolemy V- had Ptolemy VI and VII and Cleo-II
Cleo-II	184-121	Cleo-1 [mom]Married Ptolemy VI the VII [2 brothers]
Cleo-Thea	150-121	Cleo-II [mom] killed 2 husbands and the third had her drink first-she died.
Cleo-III	161-101	Married Ptolemy VI [mom's husband] then Ptolemy VIII
Cleo-IV	114-112	Cleo-III [mom]-Married Ptolemy IX [brother]
Cleo-Selene	115-103	Married Ptolemy IX [brother] then Ptolemy X
Cleo-Berenice	81-80	Married Ptolemy X [uncle and step-father] then Ptolemy XI [brother]
Cleo-V	70-68	Ptolemy IX [Dad]-Married Ptolemy XII
Cleo-VI	79-68	Cleo-V [mom]
Cleo-VII	69-30	Cleo-V[mom]-Married to 10-year-old brother, then 9-year-old brother; killed both then Mark Antony
Cleo-VIII	Died 6 BC	Daughter of Mark Antony

You would think that the Cleopatras were all beautiful so I thought it would be good to show you what they looked like.

Cleo-I Cleo-II Cleo-Thea Cleo-III Cleo-IV Cleo-Selene

Cleo-Berenice Cleo-V Cleo- VI Cleo- VII Cleo VIIII

Generally, it looks like Cleopatra VII was the most plain looking of the bunch, but there is no mistaking that these women were extremely powerful. When it comes to power, we must talk about a queen named Boadicea who also doesn't seem to have her rightful place in our history textbooks.

Britain and Boadicea

While all the Cleopatra stuff was going on, Rome was expanding to the north. For some unknown reason, the Romans wanted to take over the British Islands. You might wonder why in the world the Romans would every want this isolated place. It had no extraordinary wealth; the people stayed by themselves and were no threat. There were no significant urban areas as the people were split up into insignificant tribal units, and whenever they were attacked, the "Brits" protected their land with such a vengeance, that it took almost 100 years to subdue them [55BC to 43AD]. The Britons simply didn't want to become Romans.

Romans Were Not Stupid

Although most simply try to make you think Romans were stupid and kept on attacking the Brits just because they liked cold weather, there is a reason for the Roman tenacity. Before we get into the reasons we should look at the tenacity of the Brits to keep the Romans away. This is where a Queen named Boadicea comes in along with some other crazies. She is shown below and her followers were called Berserkers.

34

Berserkers

The battles in the British Isles brought the new word-"berserk". The word means, "Clad in bear skin". These berserk armies were almost impossible to conquer and because they fought with such fury, a new meaning arose- "crazy fighting". One thing strange is that many times, instead of wearing "bear skins", these warriors would wear "bare skin" painted blue instead of the more common Bear Skin. They probably had another name for the blue group, but the berserker name stuck.

Assassins

Along that same line, if we travel to the Middle East, we could find the drug "Hashish". During this time the armies in the area would load up on this pure form of marijuana and really fight without fear because drug wasn't against the law. The crazy fighting was similar to that of the Berserkers, but because hashish was used, the wild fighters were called the "hashshinins". Later the word was changed to "Assassin" that we use today, but I wonder how fearless the Hashshinins would have been if they wore bearskins? Can you imagine a Berserk Assassin? Now picture him naked and painted blue!

Boadicea's Revenge

Sorry for the quick trip, but we're back in Briton again. The Romans got even for the Britons going berserk by getting mean, but sometimes meanness causes more meanness. During a bloody Roman assault, one of the Iceni tribal leaders named Queen Boadicea-- [I know it's spelled a dozen different ways. I just picked one.] Anyway, she got really, really angry simply because her palace was looted, she was taken out in the streets naked and whipped with rods, and her daughters were each raped. [Go figure?] She immediately raised an army of 120 thousand soldiers and took vengeance by taking her army into Roman territory. She took over several Roman towns and she crucified or otherwise killed about 80 thousand Romans but she wasn't done there. I think it would be most reasonable to just provide what a Roman historian, Cassius Dio, had to say about her eccentricity.

"Those who were taken captive by the Britons were subjected to every known outrage. The worst most bestial atrocity committed by their captors was the following. They hung up naked the noblest and most distinguished women and then cut off their breasts and sewed them to their mouths, in order to make the victims appear to be eating them. Afterwards they impaled the women on sharp skewers run lengthwise through their entire body. "

The Romans finally ended her revenge sweep as she and her daughters evidently killed themselves to escape capture, but the sight of the Roman women being skewered would have normally made people leave this unfriendly land. The Romans stayed year after year after year. They built two walls across the entire Britannia Island to keep the Berserkers from killing anyone who came near. With almost no good reason, Romans allowed this horrible place kill soldiers and citizens every year. While textbook seem to leave out the truth, I think there was a good reason for their tenacity that is hidden or ignored from "normal History". Now, I'm going to tell you about it.

Romans Wanted America

The reason I brought up how crazy the Brits were, was to show that keeping the British Islands was "apparently" not only stupid, it was extremely difficult.

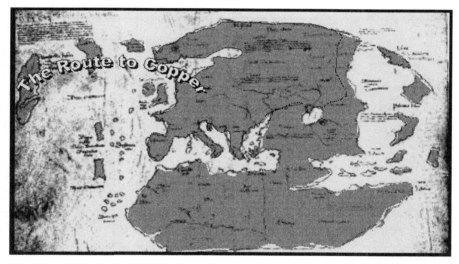

The only reason that I can figure that they would have done it is very simple. They did not have the mighty Navy of the Phoenicians and needed stepping stone islands to get to North America where vast amounts of Copper was mined by the Adena Indians. If you recall, the Aztalaneans who were the predecessor ruling class before the Adena initiated heavy mining. That was all discussed in book 5, if you want to review. The Romans must have known about the civilization and their wealth or they would not have risked so much for so little. The map above is called the Viking map. While this particular one was made a little after this period, there is strong evidence that maps to the copper rich new world was available to the Romans as the Americans were exporting the metals somewhere and the Europeans were getting copper from somewhere. When I add 2 and 2 together I get European interaction with North America. I know no one has indicated that before, but doesn't it seem reasonable?

> *The Romans were looking to take over as much of the "Wealthy World" as possible. Taking over the poor hard to handle people of the English Islands doesn't make sense, but gaining control of copper mines in America does and getting there by way of England makes sense for the Romans.*

Roman Evidence

Not only did the Romans want to come to America, they had already been to the United States area during this time. Evidence has been found to prove that their knowledge of the wealth of the Americas was first hand. Just north of Tucson Arizona, ancient Roman headgear, armor, swords, coins and other artifacts have been found. This, along with other things, shows that their attempt at taking control of the British Islands was not as stupid as we have been told.

More Coins-Other Roman coins have turned up in a garden in Oshkosh, Wisconsin, in a streambed in the Black Mountains, North Carolina, and in a field outside Phoenix City, Alabama. While each could have been a random loss of a coin collector who never tried to recover his valuable coins, the more likely answer for the large quantity of places holding these artifacts is that the Romans had been in the Americas and they had been here more than once. In fact, there is quite a bit to the history that has been robbed from our children—even with over a BILLION pounds of evidence.

Ohio Valley Copper Supplier for the world- Massive mine field cover the middle of the United States. One problem is that HUGE amounts of silver and copper are MISSING. On the ground are artifacts of a tiny portion of the manufactured items that left this area every year from about 700BC until the reconquering by the Romans to supply their needs. Left behind we find Phoenician, Egyptian, Greek, and Roman weapons and other articles that historians have been hiding so the whole Columbus story would be believed. A small sampling of what has been found is shown next.

Still more spearheads and bracelets found in the Americas bound for the Middle East.

How Much was Mined? -Michigan Alone has more than 5,000 ancient copper mining pits, some as deep as 30 feet and all so old they were filled almost to ground level with decayed vegetable matter and wind-blown soil when they were discovered in the mid-1850s. Thousands upon thousands of stone hammers used to batter pieces small enough to carry, from big, heated copper nuggets were found in and around the mining pits. It has been postulated that as many as 10,000 miners, labored some 1,000 years, in an estimated 10,000 Copper Range pits removing something like 1.5 billion pounds of copper. While that estimate might be a little high, we can certainly believe that at least 500 million pounds of copper was recovered and most of it was sold. More of the artifacts are shown below.

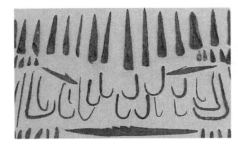 

Silver-The copper mined was not 100% copper as shown above right. The third spear head is mixed with silver in the tang while the center large one is almost 50% silver.

Spears for Everyone-The image below shows that spearheads for a number of different people were produced in the Ohio Valley. Greek style spearheads are the last ones, the middle is Phoenician, but the second one is Roman.

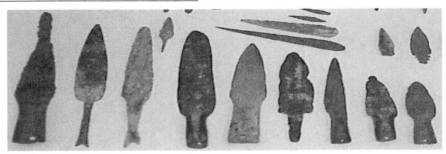

While those in America had converted to smaller battles with arrows and spears, Europe, was in the midst of its Bronze Age, fueled largely by the casting and shipping of 'oxide ingots'—with the major source of core copper still unknown to this day. With the copper they kept on producing copper, bronze and brass weapons at an alarming rate. While the Romans were trying to take control of Islands along the route to America, a baby was

40

born in Bethlehem. The baby would change humans and religion around the world. This child would reduce the image of the Nephilimic Hybrids as gods and reestablish the creator as the only true God. I'm talking about Jesus, but shouldn't there be evidence if Jesus really existed? The answer is yes.

Jesus God Incarnate

Here is where I get into some trouble. The next few pages could be considered religious ones in that they discuss an incarnated God, but like I have said many times now; science, religion, and history must all tell the same story or something is wrong with them. This discussion goes along with ALL of the elements we have been discussing from book one until now. This includes the multi-universes determined by the current scientific views, string theories, the M-theory, the Bible, many other ancient texts, and otherwise anomalous physical evidence.

Before I get into this have you ever wondered if Jesus was really God? Have you wondered why God returned to earth as a boy? Have you wondered why Jesus came to earth 2 thousand years ago rather than earlier or later? The timing seems odd at first glance and religious dogma doesn't make it any less odd. The evidence is what we should use and it strongly tells us that a very special individual was briefly on our earth about 2 thousand years ago. Given he existed, the probability of him being God is very high, but the other two questions need some explaining.

In order to get set up to advance a reasonable theory concerning the questions that many stay away from I have to step away from physical existence in this universe for a little to examine this important part of our humanity. What I think the best way to start is to describe the historical relevance of God's return as an extremely important event for humans. This will not be religious dogma but a comparative analysis of varying evidence generally presented in this work and by others.

Did Jesus Exist?

The existence of Jesus from 4BC until 30AD is critical to the historical truth and credibility of the New Testament portion of the Bible. The truth of the Biblical history is sometimes challenged, especially when the book talks about God coming down as a man.

There should be evidence outside the Bible if Jesus was a real entity and there is.

Some of the evidence has been collected here. Not only do the following excerpts talk about the existence of Jesus, but also his miraculous works. Many of the references come from Jewish historians who would be better served to ignore Jesus if they could. Just about everyone who was anyone during the Roman times had heard about and had witnessed some element of his miraculous life. Here is a sampling.

Jewish Historian Josephus- Josephus made two references to Jesus-Apostle James, *"—he is the brother of Jesus, who is called Christ", and later, "At the time there was a wise man who was called Jesus."* **[He did not identify Jesus' God status but did recognize that he was an important figure in history that really existed.]**

Thallus- He was a Roman historian from about 52AD and he noted *that darkness fell on the land at the time of the crucifixion as stated in the Bible. He wrote that an eclipse caused it.* **[This**

further adds to the mounting evidence of Jesus existence as the Bible references the same occurrence upon Jesus' death.]

Tertullian- Another Roman, this time a ruler, wrote about a report from Pontus Pilate---*"Tiberius, having himself received intelligence of Palestine of events which clearly showed the truth of Christ's divinity, brought the matter before the senate, with his own decision in favor of Christ—the senate rejected his proposal."* [Tertullian ruled around 200AD and affirmed the existence and noted evidence of divinity at the same time.]

Tertullian again- He also wrote-*"This is your carpenter's son, your harlot's son; your Sabbath-breaker, your Samaritan, your demon-possessed! This is he whom you bought from Judas. This is he who was struck with reeds and fists, dishonored with spittle, and given a draught of gall and vinegar! This is he whom his disciples have stolen secretly, that it may be said, 'He has risen', or the gardener abstracted that his lettuces might not be damaged by the crowds of visitors!"* [The document certainly shows this early Roman leader believed that Jesus did exist, was killed and the body disappeared as stated in the Bible.]

Talmud- In "Sanhedrin", one of the books of the Talmud, it States, *"On the eve of Passover, Yeshu [Jesus] was hanged -he has practiced sorcery and enticed Israel to apostasy."*---It also States that Jesus was 33 or 34 at the time. [This Jewish Law book would do better to ignore facts about Jesus, but it could not because too many Jewish people knew about him and loved him. The best they could do was to call his miraculous deeds, sorcery.]

Census- The Bible references a census at the time of Jesus birth. Historical records show that a census was ordered in Syria and Judea between 6BC and 5 AD. [Confirmation of the census adds credibility to the Biblical history.]

*Origen-*Origen was a Jewish teacher who lived in the 3rd century. He wrote, *"Jesus had come from a village in Judea, and was the* son of a poor Jewess who gained her living by the work of her own hands. She gave birth to Jesus, a bastard. Jesus, on account of his poverty, was hired out to go to Egypt. While there, he acquired certain (magical) powers which Egyptians pride themselves on possessing. He returned home highly elated at possessing these powers, and on the strength of them gave himself out to be a god." [Although there is an extensive desire to refute the divine nature of Jesus by the Jewish leaders, his capabilities were certainly known by the early Jews.]

Serapion-Mara Bar Serapion wrote around 2nd century AD. -- *"What advantage did the Athenians gain from putting Socrates to death? Famine and plague came upon them as a judgment for their crime. What advantage did the men of Samos gain from burning Pythagoras? In a moment their land was covered with sand. **What advantage did the Jews gain from executing their wise King? It was just after that their Kingdom was abolished.** God justly avenged these three wise men: the Athenians died of hunger; the sea overwhelmed the Samians; the Jews, ruined and driven from their land, live in complete dispersion. But Socrates did not die for good; he lived on in the teaching of Plato. Pythagoras did not die for good; he lived on in the statue of Hera; nor did the wise King die for good. He lived on in the teaching which he had given."* [In this passage, Mara Bar-Serapion makes these casual remarks as though everyone knew that they were truth. This is essentially saying that everyone knew that the Jews had killed their king. Of course, that "king" would have been Jesus as no "normal" king had come to his death from the people. He also generally dates the teachings of Jesus as reasonably soon after the Romans had taken control of Jerusalem.]

Ossuary Evidence-If written testimony is not enough, more physical evidence of Jesus has been found in something called an Ossuary or bone box. On a 20-inch-long stone box was inscribed the words "James, son of Joseph, brother of Jesus". I know your saying. These three names were probably extremely common so it doesn't show anything, but there are other indicators.

The Date-The Sorbonne University in Paris has authenticated the writing and dated the inscription to approximately 60AD with a high level of certainty. Both the date and the lineage match the earthly family of Jesus. In the first century A.D., common Jews followed the custom of transferring the bones of their deceased from burial caves to ossuaries similar to the one found. The practice was largely abandoned after the destruction of the Jewish Temple in 70 AD, which helped date the artifact.

Other Indications-The use of the Ossuary also aids in our determination, as this would have been a common burial element of a carpenter family. Lastly, the mention of Jesus as the brother, or half-brother in this particular case, was an unusual practice meaning that Jesus was a very well-known individual of the time. All of these things point to Jesus, the incarnate, being alive during the Bible times and recognized as a leader. [By the way the ossuary was empty if anyone wants to know.]

Possible Problem-As a matter of completeness, let me say that some experts in the Jewish community have indicated that they believe the "brother of Jesus" portion to have been added around the 2nd century or even later and was not part of the original inscription. I have no idea why the addition was done if it was done, but this is just another piece of information.

Was Jesus God Incarnate?

The evidence above only shows that Jesus existed, he had extreme magical capabilities, he lived and died in the manner described in the Bible, he disappeared after he died, and his teaching initiated the Christian faith. They do not, by themselves, provide certainty that Jesus was God. I'm not going into this detail except to say, "He was God" and make some common-sense remarks. You'll have to make up your own mind. While this in not the particular reason for this book, I must, at least, say that if Immaculate

Conception is reasonable, then God being here as a boy should also be reasonable.

Is Immaculate Conception Reasonable?

If angels are real and can take on human form then certainly the existence of God incarnate should not be difficult to fathom. There is a huge amount of evidence that has been presented in this work and many others on the existence of angels and their physical, sexual, and procreative interactions with humans. Angels had children by humans. There is much evidence to indicate that it was not only possible, but also commonplace before God put enmity between the seed of the serpent and the woman. After that time, the Nephadim had children by humans and hybrids of one sort or another had children by humans. If an angel could have offspring with humans, how easy must it be for God to have a human child?

Did Jesus Perform Miracles?

All of the writers above knew about Jesus and his miracles. Not all of them believed Jesus to be incarnated God, but all knew of his impossible magic and they all confirmed his existence. By the way, here is something to ponder. Jesus performed a tremendous number of miracles including bringing people back to life. Jesus also was, by all references, a complete pacifist. These two things made him the lowest level of threat of anyone against the king, but the king had him killed. Isn't that a strange thing? You would think that the king would have kept him around to work his miracles and increase pacifisity. While I'm not getting into this particular area, it makes little or no sense. What does make sense is that Jesus was God incarnate.

Besides the few examples above, there are many other confirming elements of God returning to earth on or about 2 thousand years ago; but WHY would he have come? Even more puzzling is, "Why did him come when he did?"

Images of Jesus- There re three images of Jesus that have survived from the time of his death. The first one below is a painting done by a woman who Jesus healed; the 2nd one is called the "Shroud of Turin" where it appears cloth covering a man was burnt just like a photograph. The last 2 were pounded into one of the first CODEX books containing Biblical details. All are from the 1st century.

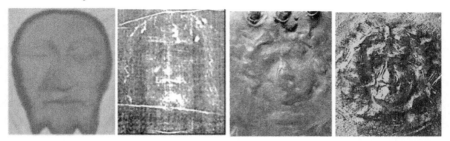

Looks like he had a large nose curly hair and trimmed beard.

Why Did God Return?

Right or wrong, details of this important part of our history has been left out of history textbooks over and over again. Here are some details that might be enjoyable to you. Hopefully, you can believe that there is good evidence that Jesus was God and he did return to Earth for some reason. Now let's see why. Sometimes people get this one twisted so I'm going to go over the reason that shows constancy. If you remember from books 1,2, 3, 4, 5, and 6, there was something that continued to be important to ALL of the various human beings throughout time besides God. That, "non-God, important thing" was identified by MANY ancient texts. The Jewish texts simply called it "the light".

Returning The "Light" Brought God Back To Earth.

While I didn't really go into what the esoteric thing called "the light" that was in the earlier books, this is where all of the discussions come together. If you remember I called the "Light" the "Heaven Key" and it is also, apparently, the key to God's return. I need to get into a little detail and back up here so we can tie everything back together. Please bear with me a little because if we look at the details it should also show us why God came back **when** he came back.

Why Did He Come When He Did?

Haven't you ever wondered why God incarnate came when he did? Why didn't he come when the Jews were oppressed? Why did he come 2 thousand years ago in the middle of the expansion of the Roman Empire? If you were thinking the Romans were part of the reason, I would beg to differ. If you have been told he came back whenever the "signs and prophecies" had been completed, that also is a bunch of bunk. Certainly, signs were completed, but so what? The signs showed God's control over things, but God came back when he did for a specific reason and it was not to make his "signs" look good. The key has to be something about the Jewish people as they were his "chosen ones" so let's investigate further.

The "Light" Overview

First let me sort of review earlier discussions that were backed up in previous books. Much of the evidence was in the form of written testimony, but it was cross-compared from histories in the Bible, ancient texts from India, Egyptian writings, and many other works from other parts of the Middle East and around the world.

Light Before the Sun-The first time we here about this "light" that wasn't a light was in the Biblical book of Genesis. That ancient book made distinction between two types of light being created. The first "light" was the weird one and a second type of light that came from the sun and the other luminaries followed it. Being told that the solar system is about 5 billion years old makes you think this non-glowing thing called "light" has been here a long time. It had nothing to do with light you could see, but we found out by comparative analysis that it had everything to do with "LIVING" in a place or universe containing Heaven. It is something needed by ANYONE who wants to live there.

During the Mesozoic Era-Ancient Humans Gain the Light-The second mention was discussions about ancient humans that lived with the dinosaurs. They gained this "light" thing after they left their "normal" human bodies in something similar to death. Several of the ancient texts indicate that the humans didn't simply die, but were somehow transformed into the angels. These angels or watchers are the same ones written about in the Biblical texts. The angels lived in heaven and later; we found out, some of them lost the capability of living in heaven because they lost the "light". Still there was no definition beyond the discussion of its loss.

120 Thousand Years Ago-Satan's Angel Followers Lose the Light-*The third mention in various ancient histories was concerning the outcome of a huge war between God, with a large group of Heaven dwellers, and Satan with another portion of the heaven dwellers. The outcome was a disaster for the Satan followers. The various texts tell us that the losers had their "light" taken away and then they could no longer live in this place called heaven. Ancient Jewish texts called the "De-lighted" angels the Nephilim. They became humans.*

40 Thousand Years ago- Adam created with this Light inside-*Now we go forward in time a long way and find a new human creation named Adam. He and his direct descendants seemed to be almost 2 entities. The carnal one would die and a second one, with this "light" thing, could go to live in heaven. It was the best of both worlds as we found out from some angels.*

30 Thousand years ago-More Angels Lose the Light-*Angels had the light, but they didn't have the carnal life. Some of the angels thought that humans had it great because they had a carnal life. Presto-Chango! A large group of angels somehow changed back into regular humans. You probably guessed it. As punishment for becoming human, they also lost the "light" and could no longer get back to Heaven. The ancient Jews knew these people in this punished group of x-angels as the Nephadim.*

20 Thousand years ago-*All the Nephilim, Nephadim, and hybrid humans try to get the light back by breeding with humans in Adam's lineage. It didn't work, but they kept on trying by all accounts.*

10 Thousand years ago-*The Bible indicates that only 8 "people" survived the flood, while around the world there is substantial* *evidence that other humans survived. We can easily assume that the Biblical history is concerning the humans in Adam's lineage. Most likely only 8 people survived that had the "light". All the other survivors would have been half-breeds. To make this a more reasonable theory we find that before the flood, those in Adam's bloodline were considered "the Chosen Ones", after the flood, we find only a small percentage of the population being considered "the Chosen Ones". If we are to believe that discussions of all of Adam's descendants being "Chosen" than we must contend that most people are not descended from Adam's or Noah's family. If that were the case ALL people would be in the "Chosen" class. The surviving Adamics in the lineage of Noah would soon be known as Jews. The others can be loosely called the Gentiles.*

*2 **Thousand years ago**- Jews started having "relations outside their bloodline. It is my strong belief that by 2 thousand years ago the Jews had completely messed up. The only thing Jews had to do was to not have sex with the half-breeds and they could go to heaven when they died. When Jesus came, just about all the Adamics had married outside their heritage at least a little bit and that was all it took. With this violation against God's instruction, the remaining "sort-of Chosen Jews" also had lost the "light".*

Some may not agree with the statements above, but they are consistent with cross-compared evidence. They point us towards a reason why God waited 40 thousand years.

Why Wait 40 Thousand Years?

One Possible Reason-For this answer we must begin by restating that some of the Nephilim survived the flood along with Noah. These guys were larger than "normal" people and they became the rulers of "normal sized people" around the world. Slowly they became too old and feeble. In Biblical texts, King David killed the last remaining group of these extremely old rulers. If you remember Goliath would have been one of the descendants of the Nephilim. The last ones identified in the Bible would have died

52

out about 1000BC or so, but others around the world may have lasted until the time that God became incarnate and Jesus lived.

Why would God wait 40 thousand years? Some may think that is an exorbitant time period, but apparently, he actually waited only until all of the direct descendants of the Nephilim were gone as was his promise to them.

Nephilimic Reign-Like I said, after the flood, and for a period of 7 thousand years prior to God's return, the Nephilim had been dying out along with their immediate offspring, as the fruit from the Tree-of-Life was no longer available to them. By several accounts the flood marked the end of that special food source we read about in Genesis. Immediately after his ominous promise of "not allowing the Nephilim entrance into heaven", God made a way for "normal humans" who began worshiping him again to enter into heaven by coming to earth he brought the "holy Spirit or Light".

If the Nephilim people did not survive the flood and did not rule the world for a long period of time, the 40-thousand-year wait doesn't make much sense does it?

Another Possible Reason for the Timing

While the statement above is the overriding element that controlled the timing of God's return there is another coincidental element that should be looked at. This is the one alluded to in the introduction. If you remember Jews were instructed to stay away from all outsiders. They were given a huge list of laws that placed grave punishments for anyone associating with non-pure Adamics. Even their relatives, the Amorites, Jebusites and others were to be killed rather than take a chance that one of the Jews might have sex with the already violated half-breeds. The simple reason why the Chosen Ones' separation was so very important and why _ALL_ of the Adamic laws were centered on separating the Adamic line from all others in the world was that the Light was resident ONLY in those few people. Since the time of Adam, 40 thousand years ago until 2 thousand years ago, non-pureblooded humans have been trying to mix with these lucky people. The Jews were instructed to kill their relatives that had mixed with non-Jewish human hybrids including the Canaanites, Amorites, Moabites, Ashurites, Malicites, Philistines and many other "cousins". The Bible doesn't go into what these unfortunate relatives had done to deserve annihilation but we were told it had something to do with sex as the covenant to hold as absolutely essential was identified as circumcision.

If a Jew mixed with a nonJew the offspring would not have the "light". Anyone, including Jews not keeping the circumcision, cannot go to heaven. Instead the spirits either drift or go to a place we call hell. I know a lot of people don't believe in this hell place or a soul, so I think a short overview is warranted, because the ancient records and common sense dictate that "the soul" of a person does something after death.

The Soul

I'm not going to simply say we have one of these soul things, but instead I will bring up mathematics. Mathematicians from around the world praised the new concept of one-dimensional strings making up our world. They called the model "The String Theory of existence". As time went on it became obvious that the basic string theory could not capture all of the anomalies in the universe so mathematicians added "Super Symmetry". This adjunct theory showed that there are at least 10 dimensions and that parallel universes make the various groups of three of more of these dimension things. Furthermore, the models show that, each of the universes affect the others. If something happens in the "heaven universe", for instance, an almost opposite thing occurs in ours. An example would be that if a large particle is made small in our universe, it forces a small particle to become large in "their" universe. Scientists are using this model to define just about everything today. The soul can be very easily defined, explained the same way. Simply put, as someone's "life" is extinguished in one universe it would be renewed in another. The mathematical model can't work if there is nothing to transfer to the other universe. I will call the life that is initiated, the soul. There is something that all of these souls don't want to do. A soul being does not want to go to any universe that is called hell.

The Hell Place

In book 2, I discussed the universality of the concept of Hell that is inhabited by Nephadim, Nephilim, their immediate descendants and quite a few other unfortunates. The concept of hell is simple. If a spirit or soul cannot go to Heaven, then wherever he may go could be considered hell. Hell could be on earth or somewhere else. In fact, there is a reasonable amount of evidence to suggest that quite a few spirits, demons, and souls still roam the earth. To them, the earth is a hell. All that sounds crazy again, but by now I'm sure you are used to that. Many times, Hell has been described as not nearly as nice as the heaven place. By many reports, hell was initially made as a place of punishment. Whatever it is, wherever it is, or for whatever reason it was established is of limited concern to those who are living; but just wait until you die and see if its existence doesn't spark your soul's interest.

Soul or No Soul That is the Question

For those that still don't believe that humans have souls and don't like the new-fangled mathematics, I can only indicate that nearly all ancient, historical records discuss this strange emanation of our person. Ignoring its possibility to eliminate the need to find out about the light/heaven key or be wary about hell may not be the wisest thing to do.

Some may believe the concept of a soul is a method for mankind to relieve tension associated with death and it is no more real than a ghost. I may tend to agree. Not because the soul is fictional, but because ghostly apparitions are probably not fictional.

Ghosts and Demons

From many sources we read about the descendants of Nephilim and gods becoming demons that must walk the world. Besides those unfortunate entities, the concept of hell does not exclude everlasting spirit-life on earth without a body. If you see a ghost----be kind. He's not having a great time.

God sent Jesus to modify the Adamic hybrids so that they would regain the "Heaven-key" and keep them from having to experience the hell place. The people needing the "light" included the now defiled Jewish race. This modification is sometimes called the fifth Human Creation, but it allows humans to travel to the Heaven Universe after death.

Apology

For those not wanting God to be in a history book, I apologize and a promise that was all as we start looking at some items that might have been left out of histories concerning Rome.

37-41AD Caligula

Probably the most hated of all the Roman emperors was gone but it was **NOT** Caligula as you might have believed from your history books. The hated leader was **Tiberius** and he was in power when Jesus was killed. Not only did Jesus' followers fear him, but also his own people despised him. Where Tiberius was definitely mean, Caligula was, at best, extremely strange. OK! He was a little mean as well; but--

The Romans did not hate Caligula.

Caligula the Beloved Ruler

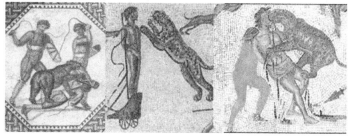 

People prayed for the new ruler that replaced Tiberius and these "normal Roman people" cried openly whenever he got sick. He was truly loved by almost all the people. This word "almost" did not include wealthy Romans.   For simple infractions some were thrown into the rink with animals to eat them alive as depicted in many murals. As such, historians don't portray him as a loved ruler because many in the ruling class hated him. Here is a quick overview of his government.

- He practiced open government,

- He lifted censorship,

- He wouldn't give the rich special privilege because of their wealth.

In fact, Caligula mocked the wealthy. You could say he even went farther than that.

Mocking the Rich

He would, on occasion, forcibly require a wealthy senator's wife to perform sex with him and either complain to the husband about how bad she was in bed or nasty she was. In one incidence, he accused the distraught husband, Marco, of the crime of pimping his unfortunate wife and ordered him to commit suicide. Several senators began to dislike him.

Sawing in Half

Still another Senator felt his wrath as the parents of a girl got to watch her sawed in half. This got to be one of Caligula's favorite past-times as shown below.

Other Entertainment-One gladiator alone was beaten up for 2 days full days. He sometimes ordered people to be <u>killed by elephants</u>. Before the elephants stomped on you sometimes, they were made to yank off an arm or so as depicted next.

Brotherly Love

While he was doing all this weird stuff, he evidently, only loved one woman. That love was Drusilla, his sister. He also had sex with his other 2 sisters, but Drusilla was special. After a while she was carrying his baby. The story goes that he tried to get the baby out of her body in a manner that killed her. When she died he declared that she was a goddess and was to be worshipped. The other two sisters were glad they didn't have to become goddesses.

Money Making

Then Caligula came up with a great way to make money. It became a capital crime not to bequeath the Emperor everything. Once the bequeathing was done, the rich began losing their lives. The rich, at least those that had escaped this new game, soon got rid of Caligula, Drusilla lost her goddess-ship, and the normal people were miserable again. The workings of the government again closed; censorship again abounded; and the rich Romans got their special privileges back. That was until a new leader got the normal people going again. This one was fat, had a huge neck and thought he could play the Lyre. He was Caligula's nephew.

54-68AD Nero

This ruler is mostly remembered for burning Rome, which he did not do by all accounts. Instead of that rubbish, we should have learned about the real Nero.

Nero

He was the ruler that <u>didn't</u> burn Rome and the ruler that was <u>loved</u> by the common people just like Caligula. Nero was a <u>comic</u> sorts. He would get on stage and act and sing for anyone who would listen. Unfortunately for him, the rich thought that the acts were demeaning to an emperor so he got into trouble.

Nero's Love Troubles

More trouble followed when he fell in love with a beautiful woman named Poppaea [middle image above]. While all his love-sickness was going on, he was having all sorts of difficulty in killing off his soon to be ex-mom, Agrippina. Poisoning and drowning didn't work but soon he completed his task. I know he was sad about the ordeal because he found a man, named

Doryphorus, that reportedly looked like his mom and he had a short sex fling with the "almost look-alike". His new boyfriend didn't like Nero giving his attention to Poppaea; so, Nero had is mom-like friend poisoned. He felt he had to so he could concentrate more on Poppaea. Even after this, Nero still had a little problem. His third wife was still around so Nero had a friend named Otho; marry his dream girl until he could get her out of the way. Well, that was a mistake because Otho fell in love with this girl who was now his wife just like Nero had ordered. Talk about a love triangle! All these twists and turns were not the end of the confusion, however.

Poppaea's Look Alike

Some histories indicate that Otho wouldn't give her back even though Nero had gone to so much trouble getting rid of her opposition. Others indicate that Nero was able to marry Poppaea. Somehow, during all this exchanging, Poppaea became pregnant with Nero's child so he kicked her in the stomach, [lightly of course], and killed her. [Sounds like Caligula and his sister doesn't it?] Nero was devastated and did the only thing he could think of. He found someone who looked almost exactly like Poppaea and they soon married [see above right], however, one problem had to be fixed before the somewhat "strange" marriage. His, soon to be, wife's penis was removed prior to the wedding. Originally a boy, Nero's newfound love, Sporus, now was an acceptable wife. You just can't have a wife with a penis, you know.

Rome Burning

Rome had burned a few years before Nero took office. In fact, the same portion of Rome would periodically burn over the years and so it was not a shock that Rome burned again while Nero was on the throne. People remember him for it, but he had nothing to do with it. He just wanted to look at his de-**penis**ated wife and remember his true love. The other thing he liked to do had to do with Jews.

Nero and the Jews

One thing that Nero is most noted for is that he tried to get rid of Jews. His form of genocide was hidden by a Jewish revolt, but it caused the extermination of 1.3 million Jews in 66AD according to the history of Josephus. I don't know if that quantity is a remarkable thing, but we must remember that the Romans didn't have all the convenient ways to kill that Hitler did. What I do know to be a remarkable thing is that there were enough Jews to allow over ½ million to be killed in another uprising 50 years later. Anyway, the Jewish population decreased during this whole time-period. Not only did the Jewish population suffer; but also, so did the Christian population. As for the Christians, there is some confusion about Christian deaths in the Great Coliseum of Rome.

The Coliseum & Christian Entertainment

You may wonder about how gross the fighting was in this huge arena, so I'll tell you. On one occasion about 3000 gladiators hacked each other to death at the same sitting at the Coliseum. The entrance ticket for that show probably cost extra but it was worth it if you liked gore. By the way, it wasn't named the Coliseum at all. A colossal statue of Nero was next to it and it sort of was called the "arena next to the colossal statue of Nero". Later the description was shortened and we have the coliseum.

No Christians at the Coliseum

Although their love of gore and torture is not easy to read about, we need to understand the level of debauchery of the Romans to understand their history. By the way, there is no record of **Christians being killed in the great coliseum** in Rome, or should I say the building next to Nero's statue, but that doesn't mean that they weren't slaughtered in other arenas and for other pleasures, it just means that the killing of Christians wasn't the main event.

Roman Candles

One day Nero came up with an unusual entertainment idea that involved Christians. During parties, he would tie them to poles and soak their cloths in oil and tar. Once the human torches were lit, his guests really had a great party while listening to the screams as shown in the following image. These would be called Roman Candles. I know I said the Romans were misunderstood, but I don't like this Nero character one bit. It seems the only two things he was good for was to kill multitudes of innocent people and to make his subjects laugh at him when he was trying to entertain them.

You would think the next image is of the bloodthirsty Nero, but it is from the Spanish Inquisition as they found out how to really torture humans.

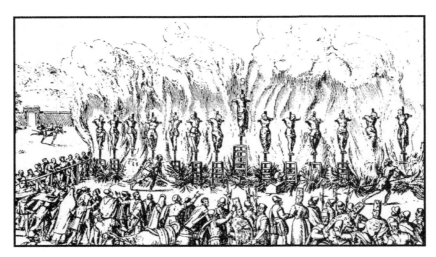

From the historian Tacitus *"-- and lamps, under the shoulders and on other tender parts of their naked bodies, after these had been cruelly lacerated with scourges or rods. This burning was done also with shavings and fagots, they (the Christians) being tied to stakes worth half a stiver. Therefore, they called the Christians drmenticii, that is, fagot people, and semissii, that is, half stiver people; because they stood fastened to half stiver stakes, and were thus burned with the slow fire of fagots.*

Roman poets Juvenal and Martial said it this way-*Of those who were burned, some were tied or nailed to stakes, and held still by a hook driven through the throat, so that they could not move the head when the pitch, wax, tallow, and other inflammable substances were poured boiling over their heads, and set on fire, so that all the unctuous matter of the human body flowing down made long, wide furrows in the sand of the theatre. And thus, human beings were lighted as torches, and burned as lights for the wicked Romans at night.*

The historian Tertullian gave us even more detail showing how frequently this stunt was accomplished. , --- *the Romans wrapped them in a painful or burning mantle, which they, wound around their hands and feet, in order to melt the very marrow in their bones.*

He also made crucifixion popular. I'm not talking about the way you see it on TV. He would hang people upside down and sometimes roast their heads in fire or put heavy weights tied to their bodies to give more pain. The image following may give you an idea of how these demons worked.

Crucifixions were everywhere, hangings, burnings, animal rippings, and the like. Another Emperor was very similar on the funny side. Like Nero's followers, his subjects laughed at him and he loved to perform in the Coliseum. His name was Commode.

Emperor Commode (180-192A.D.)

It seems that most of the Roman leaders were characters, but it is not my intention to repeat history that can be gotten from any other book. In addition to the antics of Nero and Caligula, Commode had a level of similarity and antic-ness, so it is appropriate that he should be addressed here. His name was actually Marcus Aurelius Commodus Antoninus, and he was the son of the Emperor Marcus Aurelius and he was given the title Caesar when he was 5 years old. In the Latin way he was soon known simply as Commodus, or Commode if was Americanize it. When he was 17 he became an Emperor of an empire that had once been called Rome. I know you probably haven't heard this before, but he changed the name of Rome to the **Colony of the Commode** [Actually, its exact name was Colonia Lucia Annia Commodiana.]. Then he decided to change all the months of the year to portions of his family name, so January became Lucius. It was followed by Aelius, Aurelius, Commodus, Augustus, Herculeus, Romanus, Exsuperatorius, Amazonius, Invictus, Felix, and finally, Pius. Commodians [some call them Romans] didn't mind the confusing months and they liked him because he gave them things that he typically took from the ruling class. Guess what! The ruling class didn't like him at all.

In order to get love, Commode had his own group of 300 girls and 300 boys that he kept close. Some say the number was higher, but the higher numbers start sounding like he was a deviate so I'm sticking with the minimums.

Commode god

He thought of himself as a descendant of Hercules so June became the "month of Hercules". As a descendent of Hercules, he made people address him as a god.

Commode As A God

He put action behind his words and would fight gladiators, bears, and ostriches in the arena to show everyone how powerful he was. Oh, did I mention that the gladiator opponents had wooden weapons? He beat them all.

He began the slow process of decriminalizing the Christian faith during his reign and giving back some of the conquered territories, so he wasn't completely caught up in his fantasy world and many people didn't mind being Commodians, but his time was not to last long. Some didn't think of him as a god or like his inability to govern so they finally did away with him and the "Empire of the Commode" became Rome again. Afterwards, the months were renamed with the more familiar titles so we still have June.

You would think that his death would stabilize the empire, but, instead, 5 "emperors" were successively brought to the throne and then overthrown [killed] within a period of about one and a half years after his death so I guess the Commodians liked Commode better than the later rulers. Even if they did like Commode, I don't feel that way. Just thinking about the commode emperor makes me feel dirty and I want to take a bath.

67

Bath, Lead, Miles, and Ships

Unfortunately, we cannot go away from the commode as we look at the Roman effect on history. The Romans were weird, mean, and despicable, but they helped mold human society with a number of things. Although the next few items are not the major molding elements, what they do show is a molding of history to provide desired outcome rather than truth. Historians histories should always be suspect [except for mine]. Some suspected historical items are "commode use [in keeping with the previous section]; bathing or not bathing; lead poisoning, making of the mile, and making a strong Navy. Let's start with the commode.

Roman Commodes

Romans were famous for their baths, so the question might be, "Did they take a bath in the public bath?" One answer is No! One of the most predominant things in the Roman Baths was the toilet. Look at this community bath house accessory. I don't mean one toilet, I mean dozens. Just think what the placed was like on a Saturday night. Now that is what I call civilized.

69

Romans Bathe

Oh Yeah! There were non-toilet areas as well, but those community areas were not used for bathing either. Those areas were for scraping. The method used by the Romans to get rid of the grime of the day was to smear oil on their bodies and scrape the oil off. They had special tools made up to make the scrape job a wonderful experience. Below is a picture showing a typical set of scrapers and an oil jar that would accompany someone to the "Bath/scrape".

This whole communal toilet and scraping thing was common everywhere, in fact the picture of the toilet on the previous page was actually found in Ephesus, Turkey during the Roman occupation. Similar scrapers were found in the bathhouses of ancient Mohenjo Daro. This Pakistani city was a commerce center some 6 thousand years ago, so we know that scraping was considered bathing for centuries. After a communal toilet break and a good scraping, the Romans could drink some lead.

Roman Lead

Lead poisoning was rampant in Rome and they didn't even know it. In a matter of only a couple of hundred years, the rich women became infertile from drinking from lead goblets and the upper classes simply died out. The rich also used lead to sweeten foods and cure diarrhea. Sometimes the cure is worse than the disease. In this case, the death that cured diarrhea is similar to the old Monty Python routine where an ingrown toenail doctor used dynamite to cure his victims—many were missing but believed to have been cured. In the case of the Romans, their diarrhea was also believed to have been cured. Between their bathing and lead drinking, the Romans walked a lot and decided to come up with the "Mile".

The Mile Was Invented

Americans adopted miles from the Romans and it's a good thing, because now that everyone in the world uses kilometers, the Americans have the only reasonable measurement tool. Many know that the word "mile" comes from the Latin word "Mille", which means thousand, and the Mille for distance was determined by steps. The question is, "How many steps are there in a "Mille". If you said 1 thousand, it would make too much sense. In fact, mile means 2 thousand steps, with a "two step space" equaling a little over 5 feet. After standardizing the "2 step" space to be 5.28 feet, the 5280 feet measurement was formalized. Now we have an exact and useful tool. Below are the things that can be converted into the fabulous mile [2 thousand steps] standard that everyone should convert to.

Roman Mile			
British Mile	1.15152	10,000 spans	1.42045
Nautical Mile	1.15078	10,000 yards	5.68182
10,000 Palms	4.73185	1,000 rods	3.12500
Kilometer	0.62137	100 skiens	6.81818

Maybe I was wrong. The "mile" is not a very good measurement tool, but one of the other things Rome was famous for was its war-ship.

Roman Warships

Another sort of death trap was a Roman War-ship. All of the movies are totally wrong about chained men being whipped to row faster in the not too efficient Roman Galleys. On the Galley ships, only "free" men rowed because they were substantially more reliable than slaves. No chains and no slaves were used. Our "normal" history books soften the details and distort ideas to bring out issues and at the same time this renders the stories almost useless as history. This may be one of those "rare?" examples of historians trying to show how terrible a slave's life was in Rome. Just think of being chained to an oar and whipped to bring you up to ramming speed. ----never happened-- What did happen was the building of a huge ship.

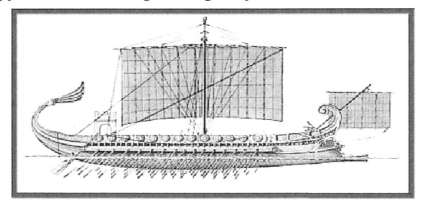

The Roman Mistake

By this time, the Greeks and Phoenicians had standardized the ship-world with what is called the "Triere" [Three-er] as shown above. For power, it consisted of three rowers per position, per side; with about 28 positions. It could be driven at speeds up to about 7 knots with its typical rowing team of 170. The Romans were better than the Greeks so they invented the "Fortier". This monstrosity had 10 men per oar and 4 layers of rowers. The huge ship was 420 feet in length, 57 feet wide and carried about **4 thousand rowers** wielding 50-foot long, lead weighted oars. Of course, it was almost totally useless if you wanted to turn, so they went back to "three-ers" after being laughed at by the other nations and destroyed in ANY battle waged with the 40er.

Below is a typical Triere next to a depiction of the Fortier.

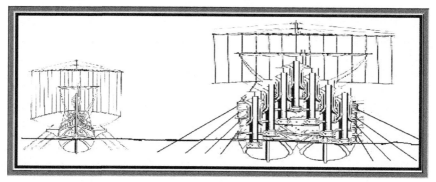

Romans had a bad Navy, but their Army was great. Another group also distinguished itself as having a great and a horrible Army.

434-453 AD Attila the Hun

OK! Romans really had a bad Navy, but their Army was almost unbeatable until the Huns came. These were the last days of the Roman Empire, and Attila the Hun was quietly killing and taking over Europe. Then he turned towards Rome, but before he went there, Attila had made a path of terror unsurpassed in recent history. Not because of the huge area of conquest, but because he would remove the heads of the unfortunate losers and stack them up into huge "Head Hills" outside a city that he had taken over. When the smell got too bad he went to another town. The Romans defeated him finally, because they had good motivation and Europe finally quit smelling so bad. I have no idea if the stories about him dying of a nosebleed on his wedding night are true, nor do I know how he would have gotten such a thing.

A pleasant killing machine. he is shown above left with horns, but, I think that the horns were added by the Romans just for the picture on one of their coins. He, sort of, looked like our Devil image, didn't he?

74

European Dark Age

The Roman Empire started falling apart. Its collapse was hurried by a little thing we call the European Dark Ages. Like the beginnings of the previous Dark Ages, from 536 to 550 AD there was another "no-growth" period, as recorded by tree rings like we discussed in book 6. It wasn't a terrible Dark Age as Dark Ages go, but it is the one we most remember, so, for us, it seemed to be unbearably terrible. Not only was it famous for the Black Death (The Justinian Plague) and very limited advancement in science, but what we don't typically realize or discuss is that the sky was dark in the day time after many meteors fell on the Earth. I know you haven't heard of the meteors, but dust from the impacts must have covered much of the world, just like most of the other Dark Age times. Here are a few of the recorded observations:

Flavius Cassiodorus [Roman]- Cassiodorus was an Italian historian who wrote about conditions that he experienced during the year 536AD: *"The Sun seems to have lost its wonted light, and appears of a bluish color. We marvel to see no shadows of our bodies at noon, to feel the mighty vigor of the Sun's heat wasted into feebleness, and the phenomena, which accompany an eclipse prolonged through almost a whole year. We have had a summer without heat. The crops have been chilled by north winds, [and] the rain is denied."*

Procopius [Roman]-Another Italian wrote a similar description, *"During this year a most dread portent took place. For the Sun gave forth its light without brightness...and it seemed exceedingly like the Sun in eclipse, for the beams it shed were not clear."*

Lydus [Roman]-   A third Italian told a similar story concerning the year 536AD, *"The Sun became dim...for nearly the whole year...so that the fruits were killed at an unseasonable time."*

Michael the Syrian- The Syrians had the same experience and Michael wrote this, *"The Sun became dark and its darkness lasted for eighteen months. Each day it shone for about four hours, and still this light was only a feeble shadow...the fruits did not ripen and the wine tasted like sour grapes."*

Chinese historical records of 540AD-"The stars were lost from view for three months. Dragons fought in the pond of the K'uh -- They went westward--In the places they passed, all the trees were broken--" **[While this identifies the dust covered sky and broken trees, probably, from the meteor strike]** Other records indicate that the light from the Sun dimmed, the expected rains did not eventuate, and snow was seen in the middle of summer. Famine was widespread, and in the midst of the turmoil, the Emperor abandoned the capital.

Middle Ages Manuscript- "Chronicon Benedicti" "In the year of 921, in the time of lord John X was pope, in the 7ᵗʰ years of his pontificate, a sign was seen. About that time, many stones were seen to fall from heaven near the city of Rome—in the village called Narnia-The largest among all the many stones fell into the river Narnia—and can be seen protruding to a height of about one cubit above the river water." [Although this document seems to indicate that the huge meteor storm occurred about 900AD, more than likely, it is actually talking about the storm that occurred in 536AD.]

Crabby Possibility

Not everyone believes that the above descriptions occurred from a huge meteor storm. Although I believe that this hypothesis is unworkable, it is believed by some that when the crab nebula was formed around 500 AD. That the event was so bright that it would have been visible in the daylight and would have cast a shadow during the night. There is a slim possibility that this event could have happened to make the sky strange while the droughts that occurred just happened to happen about the same time. Again, I think that the probability is extremely low and it would not provide a reason for the droughts, darkness in the daytime, and famine. It is data, however, that should be considered.

500-1000AD Byzantine

The darkness and accompanying famine didn't destroy everything in the Roman Empire, but instead the defeat of Attila and other marauders was not decisive. The Romans began losing control. Along with the Huns, other factions began to take back pieces of land and make their own little kingdoms. Rome was splitting into several pieces. One of the larger kingdoms was sort of centered around Christianity. The "heart" of the Christian kingdom at that time was in Byzantium [now called Istanbul], so this kingdom was called the Byzantine Empire. Really named Constantinople, who would want an Empire called the Constantinoplian Empire. The Christian kingdom actually had two "centers" during this time. Each one was trying to outdo the other. One was the Constantinople city while the other was in Rome.

The Byzantine Empire wasn't an empire in the big sense; in fact, the people of Rome and Constantinople were always bickering. Each group believed they were the Christian center of the world. In addition to being the Byzantine Empire Era, the whole time between 500 and 1000 AD was filled with people trying to suppress knowledge. The zealots of this time period believed it was a requirement of the Bible to eliminate anything that was not church-like or at least what, they believed, church-like should be and yet, the one thing that was holding the European people together was this new Bible.

Fix the Bible-Each person's "Bible" was different so large groups of well-meaning clergies tried to establish which of the hundreds of "Holy" books that had surfaced should be read and which ones should be destroyed. Many of the writings were contradictory to one another so some of the deletions were obvious, but the job of finding the "Divine Ones" was an almost impossible job. In fact, it took over 1600 years to sort of settle on a good group of books.

The Bible and Canon

I know that some are irritated that I keep using Biblical texts to define our history and others are upset that many of the "Biblical references" are not part of what many consider to be canon to the Bible, so I thought it would be best to discuss what ancient Jewish books were considered "good" and which ones were either "not required" or "bad". Don't worry, I'm not going to discuss all 600 books. Instead, the way I have chosen to do that is by examining the canonization sequence.

70-1661 AD- Ecumenical Councils

Even though there were discussions before his time, Constantine the Great [307-337], brought major emphasis to his quest for the "True" Bible. He brought together the best religious minds from around Europe and attended the truth-determining sessions called "ecumenical councils" which were designed to determine which writings were sacred, which ones were just nice to have around, and finally, which ones should not be read at all.

The first council was held around 70 AD, but the bickering would last for about 16 hundred years before a set of books was determined to be acceptable to a large quantity of Clerics. This all-encompassing collection of books, put together in 1661. The English version was known as the King James Bible. Certainly, there were Bible collections before that time as the majority of the confusion was settled by the 4th century, but still some questions lingered and that is what I want to focus on. Even after 1661, there were major modifications. Changes to the American version of the King James Bible happened as late as 1827.

1827 Canon-This 1827 version is the one generally thought of as canon by many, but it has even changed since that time as different translations such as the Revised Standard Version of the

Bible, published in 1957, generally, reintroduced books that were taken out in 1827.

Book Modification-Keeping the salvation story intact while eliminating the other elements did not go together quite as nicely as you would think. Five of the books, which were determined to be worthy of canon were only accepted after they were hacked up and some of the chapters were removed. The books Psalms, Ezra, Nehemiah, Daniel, and Esther were longer in their original version but now we have the Reader's Digest version. The book of Baruch was also dissected before finding favor with many. The books of Ruth and Song of Solomon, which never mentioned God were accepted as canon right away, but the books of Enoch and Jasher, which were quoted throughout the Bible and, by the sheer quantity of copies found at the Dead Sea site, were the most read books in earlier days were left out after 400AD except for the particular "canon" used for the Ethiopian Bible. It is believed that many of these books were simply unavailable to the clerics during this recognition time and were left out, not because of incorrect information, but because they were unknown.

Salvation Story Survived

It was an extremely difficult task and some of the historical components were removed even though many believed them to be worthy of incorporation into the final "Canon". There is no question in my mind that the current versions of the Bible tell the complete story of salvation, and most Christians believe that the discussions and extractions made by the various ecumenical councils of the Bible were God inspired. This truth would only be with respect to the Biblical discussions concerning salvation [reception of the heaven-key] as it is the major reason for the Bible in the first place.

Old Testament Canon

Anyway, here is a general list of books removed from the Old Testament portion of our "current" Bible. This of course, does not

80

include any of the books of the Gnostics or any other book that was not originally accepted as canon by one or more of the discussion groups. Even the books that were to remain were different depending on particular religious sects as shown below. While the Ethiopic Church accepted almost all of the books shown, the Eastern Orthodox only accepted those identified as Apocrypha, the Catholic Church used its own set of books. Some of the Protestant religions finally removed all of the books listed below. In this set of books I have used information from some of these removed books to support some of the Historical elements of the past. The "Biblical books" used in this history were Sirach, Baruch, II and IV Esdras, the removed chapters of Daniel, Jubilees, Jasher, Enoch I, and Enoch II. Although the books have no substantial significance with respect to the main theme of the Bible, they do provide us with additional information about our very ancient history and should not be ignored for those elements. Other works used in this history were not considered canon for one reason or another, but in many cases that reason was that the particular texts were lost to the world for a time and could not be considered. Certainly, that is the case with the "Book of Secrets", "Book of Giants", and the texts dealing with characteristics of Adamic humans, which I presented in their entirety to bring out aspects of our history.

The following table shows books not found in the American version of King James Bible but were considered canon at one time or another as shown below. Please note the canon list of the original King James Bible. A "D" indicates that the book was "Disputed" by some clerics but stayed in the canon. The "L" indicates that these books were probably lost to those considering canon.

My suggestion is to read all 66 books.

List of Canonized Old Testament Books

	Vulgate Bible 90AD	Alexandria 200AD	Origen 235AD	Aquilies 380AD	Jerusalem-451AD Eastern Orthodox	Council of Trent-1560AD**	1611 King James Bible	Revised Standard 1957	Ethiopic Bible-1300	1827 version KJ
39 books of 1827 Bible	A	A	A	A	A	A	A	A	A	A
Additions to Esther					A	A	A	A	A	
Psalm 151	A	A	A	A	A	A			A	
Psalm 152-155				A						
I-II Maccabees	A	A	A	D	A	A	A	A	A	
III-IV Maccabees	A	A	A	D	A	A	A		A	
Ecclesiasticus/Sirach	A	A	A	D	A	A	A	A	A	
Tobit	A	A	A	A	A	A	A	A	A	
Judith	A	A	D	D	A	A	A	A	A	
Wisdom of Solomon	A	A	A	D	A	A	A	A	A	
Baruch	A	A	A	A	A	A	A	A	A	
Letter of Jeremiah	A	A	A	A	A	A	A	A	A	
Esdras III& IV	A	A	A				A	A	A	
Daniel 3:24-90 *	A	A	A	A	A	A	A	A	A	
Daniel 13 &14**	A	A	A	A	A	A	A	A	A	
Prayer of Manasseh	A	A	A	A	A		A	A	A	
Enoch I/II	A	A	A	L	L	L	L	L	A	
Jubilees	A	A	A	L	L	L	L	L	A	
Ascension of Isaiah	A	A	A						A	
Assumption of Moses		A	A							
Matthias			A							
Apocalypse of Elijah			A							
Jannes & Jambres			A							
Prayer of Joseph			A							

*Called "Prayer of Azariah" and "The Song of 3 Young Men"
**Commonly called "Susanna", and "Bel & the Dragon"
A= Accepted D= disputed S= secondary importance L=Lost

New Testament Canon

The New Testament fared no better than the Old Testament during these many sessions, but it was different in that before 140AD the collection of books was substantially less filled than what we see today. The books were still being written as the councils were trying to establish canon [truth]. By 200AD it had expanded to a huge list and then the various councils of the day started throwing some of the books away to purify the New Testament. The list of qualified books was reduced to those shown and then came the real fun of each group arguing about which ones should be kept from the short list and which one of these remaining books should be "canon". Of that list, there was never a unanimous consensus except for the first seven books. The remaining 30 were in one day and out the next.

Questionable Texts

The ones which engendered the most bickering were the books of James, 2 Peter, 2 John, 3 John, Hebrews, Jude, and the Revelation of John. The majority prevailed so they stayed as books of this New Testament, but generally they were considered to be of secondary worth until 1827. At that time, the King James and the German version of Bibles both accepted the secondary books as worthy. Notice also that the last portion of 1 John, Luke, John and portions of Acts were all added about a thousand years ago and were not in the original translations.

The list below shows the various examples of canon. The layout of the table is slightly different than what you might be used to as the list is from "most accepted" to "least accepted" of the various books being considered as canon. From left to right is generally aligned by time period. There were other books accepted by one group or another, but these are the most widely accepted.

My suggestion is to read all 38 books.

List of Canonized New Testament Books

Canonized New Testament Writings	Marcion-140AD	Irenaeus-180AD	Muratorian-200AD	Eusebius-325AD	Athanasius-300AD	Claromontus 400AD	Clement Alexandria	Ethiopian-modern	Catholic-modern	Nestorian [Syrian]	John Calvin Bible	Luther Bible 1541	Karlstadt Bible	King James 1611	New King James 1827
Romans, Ephesians,	A	A	A	A	A	A	A	A	A	A	A	A	A	A	A
Corinthians, Galatians,	A	A	A	A	A	A	A	A	A	A	A	A	A	A	A
Luke, Thessalonians	A	A	A	A	A	A	A	A	A	A	A	A	A	A	A
Colossians	A		A	A	A	A	A	A	A	A	A	A	A	A	A
Matthew, Mark, John ,		A	A	A	A	A	A	A	A	A	A	A	A	A	A
Acts, I & II Timothy,		A	A	A	A	A	A	A	A	A	A	A	A	A	A
Philippians		A	A	A	A	A	A	A	A	A	A	A	A	A	A
1 John		A	A	A	A	A	A	A		A	A	A	A	A	A
Titus		A	A	A	A	A	A	A	A	D	A	A	A	A	A
Philemon	A			A	A	A	A	A	A	A	A	A	A	A	A
I Peter		A		A	A	A	A	A	A		A	A	A	A	A
Hebrews *		A		S	A	A	A	A	A	A	A	S	D	A	A
John's Revelation *		A	A	S	A	A	A	A	S		S	S	D	S	A
2 John *		A	A	S	A	A	A	A	S		S	S	D	S	A
Jude * & James*			A	S	A	A	A	A	S		A	S	D	S	A
II Peter, 3 John				S	A	A	A	A	S		S	A	D	S	A
Epistles								A	A	A					
Shepherd of Hermas		A		D		A	A	A							
Solomon's & Peter's Revelation, Barnabas	A		A	D		A	A								
Clement I&II				D			A	A							
Epistle of Eusebius							A	A							
III Corinthians				D			A								
Gospel of Peter				D			A								
Thomas, Matthias				D											
Apostolic Constitution										A					
Mark 16:9-20										A	A	A	A	A	A
John 7:53-8:11										A	A	A	A	A	A
1 John 5:7											A	A	A	A	A
Western Acts additions				D						A	A	A	A	A	A

***Referred to as "Deuterocanonical Works"** or of the second canon.

A= Accepted   D= disputed texts   S= of only secondary importance.

965-1014 Constatinoplean War

The Byzantine world was crumbling during the canonization of the Biblical text. Even though the Byzantine Empire was starting to collapse, Basil II of Constantinople was doing well but was warring with the Bulgarians. In fact, the two countries had been fighting for 40 years. In one battle in 1014, Basil's team became victorious and took 15 thousand prisoners. With a new innovation in fighting, the Constantinopleans took the prisoners and set them all free to win the war. Oh! I forgot, before they set them free all but 150 ex-prisoners had been blinded while the remaining ones had been blinded in only one eye. The returning "freed Army" was too much for the Bulgarians to handle and the king died from seeing the sight of the sightless soldiers. Basil II became the "Slayer of the Bulgarians".

If you recall I called the people who had obtained the "light" a 5th creation of humans rather than calling them Christians. This is one of the problems with a name as blinding thousands of men does not seem "5th Creation-like" to me while it was done in the name of Christianity.

622-1100AD The "Great" Crusade Fallacy

The thing that is not discussed in our History textbooks concerning this horrible time is that the State Church of Catholicism was not invading Jerusalem to make everyone Christian, they were trying to keep the Muslim hordes from taking any more of Europe. To give you an understanding of the underlying reason for the Crusades, here are the main Crusades that began in 622 to take over the world. I believe that if I had the time, **I could show that the Muslims, in their western imperialist, colonialist, bloody conquests just prior to the Catholic Crusades, killed two to three times as many Christians as the Christians killed Muslims in all of the Crusades combined** so don't go punishing the Quasi-Christian Crusaders without knowing the whole story. Here is a partial list of the Muslim Crusades.

622-634- Arabian Jihad-Mohammed's reign of terror included destruction of those in the Sinai Peninsula as he forced conversion to his new religion. Many died and many were enslaved.

634-651-Persian Jihad- This bloody "Holy War" included the takeover of Iran, Pakistan, and beyond. Many died and many were enslaved. Most were Jewish and those pagans still worshiping the moon goddess Allat'. Muslims sort-of worshipped the same goddess except Mohammed changed Allat's name and sex from female to male calling him Allah'. He kept the sign of the crescent moon and star of the goddess Inanna so conversion would be easier and he kept the sacred black meteorite stone that the faithful are supposed to kiss one time in their life.

634-1453-Byzantine Jihad- This Jewish and Christian focused Jihad included takeovers of Jerusalem, Syria, and Constantinople. This lasted for 800 years of almost continuous fighting. Many died and many were enslaved.

636-1018-Indian Jihad – This was a bloody jihad to rid the world of Hindu and Buddhists. Many died and many were enslaved.

640-700-North African Jihad- including Tunisia, Libya and Egypt. Many died and many were enslaved.

651-751- Fertile Crescent Jihad- including Iraq and Turkey which showed some of the bloodiest wars. Many died and many were enslaved. Many were Christians.

711-900- First Spanish Jihad- The takeover of Spain and Portugal; this was followed by 200 years of killing to hold onto the countries. Many died, heads were removed and parades showed off the lust for conquest, and many were enslaved including the daughters and queens of the rulers.

720-732 French Jihad- This effort finally forced massive defeats and it increased the unity of the European block of countries.

812-940- Italian Jihad- This included the takeover of Corsica, Sicily, and Italy up to the Roman Catholic City. Many died and many were enslaved.

Muslim history states- *"Almost all the people in the countries they took control of between 700 and 1100 AD wanted to become Muslim and they entered peacefully".* I think some short descriptions of the "peaceful Muslim-ation of Europe will help you.

Muslimation of Spain-711-1031-Within 200-300 years of the initial invasion in 711, over 80% of Spain's population was

Muslim, numbering over 5 million people. We are told most of these people were originally from Spain but DNA tells us a different story. While the northern sections of Spain have populations with a high percentage of the European [R1b] mutation, when we look at the southern, Andalus/Muslim sections, we find almost exclusive Arabian heritage as the original Spanish people were eliminated.

1096-1277 Eight fight back Crusades

If you remember Christian faith is not good for war as Jesus commanded all followers to "turn the other Cheek". That part of the Bible was crossed out by many in the State religion of Catholicism. While not following most of the commands of Jesus, this group cannot be the representative of Christians as the Crusades had nothing to do with turning the other cheek as the entire European group of nations began to fight back and regain their homeland. Shortly after the almost complete takeover of Spain, someone probably stood up and said. "Why don't we kill all of the Moslems?" That address started the Holy Wars and later, this same group, decided that the Jews would be nice to kill as well. These "Holy Wars" were utterly ridiculous. Rape, pillage and plunder were all advanced in the name of Christianity. [Again, not the 5th creation type Christians.] This overview might give you an appreciation of this grand set of wars that occurred over this 200 year period.

*The Love Mongols Crusade-*In the first crusade, 300 thousand knights temporarily took Jerusalem away from the Moslems. It was pretty easy because the Moslems were fighting the Mongols and had no time to fight the clumsy metal laden knights. Hurray for the Mongolians!!

*The No Mongol Crusade-*The second crusade tried to take Jerusalem again and it was a failure. Part of the reason for Crusaders loosing was armor. Too heavy to fight in the mud, the whole armor thing should have been rethought. A second reason for the heavy warriors loosing was the Mongolians were taking a break.

The Fruitless & Glorious Crusade-Richard the Lionhearted of England was in the third one. He won a couple of battles, was captured, ransomed, and returned to England. One book claimed this crusade to be glorious but fruitless. The crusaders still wore the Armor and one of Richard's winning times was when he took 3 thousand Moslem captives, and slaughtered them including all the women and the children. We'll call it a glorious failure and call Richard the Glorious King of England, even though he never even learned the written English text.

The Wrong City Crusade-In 1204 we have the 4th crusade against the wrong town. The crusaders ran out of money and couldn't make it to Jerusalem to fight, so that went to Constantinople instead, and sacked that city, even though no one wanted the crusaders there and the various religious elements of the city were operating in great harmony before the crusading invaders came. Even though it was stupid, was the wrong objective, no one wanted them there, and many died, we'll call it a glorious victory.

The Kill Everyone Crusade-The fifth one was an utter failure. Mongolians had shifted their interest towards Europe so they were no help against the Moslems. Some say the crusade was not a complete failure, for in 1209 some of the French crusaders took over the town of Beziers. Unfortunately, the winners could not tell who were Christians and who were the hated Jews and Moslems. The answer was simple. They killed every man woman and child and let God sort out those who were the infidels. The victorious French rejoiced at their "Holy War".

The Kill a Jew Crusade-The 6th crusade recaptured Jerusalem even though the people of Jerusalem didn't want the crusaders there. One difference was noted in this great war; during this struggle the crusaders tried to exterminate the Jews. These holy soldiers had trouble keeping their swords sharp because they had so many Jews to slaughter. When they were through, over ten thousand innocent Jewish settlers were slaughtered. Another victory!

The 22 Year Crusade-The 7th crusade was a really long one. It lasted 22 years and was a failure, but I'm sure it was glorious.

The Children's Crusade-The last noble crusade was fought with children, 50 thousand of them. This is going to be a shock. The children lost and many were sold into slavery.

Hip Hip Hurray-So what we find is that all 8 major Crusades against whoever were glorious. Sometimes they were glorious in defeat. sometimes they were glorious at the wrong town, and sometimes glorious in defeat again. It almost sounds like the people were fighting for glory rather than the things that a crusader should kill people for. I especially liked the children war. The whole time they were at war they probably chanted "Hip-hip-hurray". If you ever wondered why someone would say such a thing, it comes for those crusaders. The word HIP comes from the initials of "Hieroso Iyma est Pedita" [Jerusalem has fallen]. The "hurray" part is actually older and come from the Slavic language for "To Paradise". Therefore, you and I are really saying "Jerusalem has fallen, on to paradise." What a thing to say at a ball game! One group that didn't say HIP HIP Hurray was the Mongols. Not because they originally liked the Moslems, but because they saw a bigger picture. Before we get to the wonderful Mongols, let's go north for a second and quickly investigate how democracy was finding itself in England. The document we all remember is the Magna Carta.

1215 Magna Carta

This was a great document. Right?? We are told it was, but we are not told what it was about nor are we told the fact that it was only recently found by accident when a librarian was rummaging through some old documents. It wasn't a great or even a significant document or it would not have been lost for hundreds of years. Here are a few elements they seemed to miss in our Histories.

- Trial by combat was a hideous way to die, so the Magna Carta said that was fine.

- Worse than that was trial by ordeal. Dropping someone in a vat of boiling tar to see if the innocent survived was considered fair in the eyes of the Magna Carta directives.

- Trial by jury was the one you and I were told about and it was another neat trick. The problem is that a jury only tried crimes of 17 percent of the people the other 83 percent were called serfs and they were considered below the law.

- By the way, King John never signed the Magna Carta. He did place his seal on it, but that is not the same. Even if it was "stamped" as a law, in all likelihood it was NEVER considered law and was simply put on a shelf to fade away in time. At no time was there any indication of it being used at any trial or government discussion.

NEVER!

Also, by the way, John was not the enlightened despot that would come up with a great liberty expanding document anyway.

- He lost the Lormandy War and fled the battlefield as his men died and he murdered his cousin Arthur and kept Arthur's sister in prison for 40 years.

- He stole another man's wife and used hostages for the sake of fidelity and then killed them for the sake of fun.

- Speaking of fun, he locked up a "friend's" wife and child until they starved to death.

Now that we understand how bad the Magna Carta really was, let's move back to Europe again and try to fight Genghis Khan.

1200AD Black Death

Now that England is civilized let's discuss the Khans of Mongolia and see how civilized they were. Genghis, Ogedei, and Khubilai [Shown below] all shared a heritage that has been glossed over by many. They weren't the nicest people, but they were important to our history. After all, they invented germ warfare.

1206-1227 Genghis Khan

His real name was Temujin and he was said to have been the greatest military strategist of all time, but was Genghis Khan a nice guy? In 1206, at a meeting of all the tribal leaders, he was proclaimed Genghis Khan, which means "Ruler of All Within the Oceans". Genghis Khan made military service mandatory for males between the ages of fourteen and sixty. [**What a draft**].

The crusaders loved him during the first six Crusades. The diversion of Genghis Khan fighting the Moslems allowed the Crusaders some possibility of victory between 1095 and 1229. The Europeans praised the name of Genghis Khan.

The Khan Turns Toward Europe-After the sacking of Cracow in 1241, the prevalent Mongol admiration that the Crusaders had, sort of, changed as he went for Europe. Genghis Khan killed hundreds of thousands of people, but his offspring would make the really big splash. After killing as many as he could, Genghis Khan died in 1227. Forty virgin women and forty horses followed

Genghis into his tomb, which remains undiscovered to this day. [**I don't know if the virgins wanted to go or not, but they went just the same.**]

1227-1260 Ogedei Khan

Ogedei and his successors were addicted to drinking alcohol as he took on the Moslem faith, but he still was able to make a new killing record. He was said to have killed 14 million people to promote his newly found religion with Mohamed as the prophet. To put that in perspective, Hitler killed an estimated 6 million Jews.

1260-1294 Kubilai Khan

By the reign of Khubilai Khan (Genghis's grandson) in 1260, the Mongol Empire stretched nearly from ocean to ocean: from the Pacific to the Black Sea and Persian Gulf, from Siberia to Burma and the Himalayas. The Mongols fought like they hunted. Warriors ate dogs, wolves, rats, and lice, [I have no idea how you would eat a lice-possibly with a tiny, tiny spoon.] and, when necessary, they drank the blood from an incision cut into the throat of their horses and they didn't wear the heavy armor of the doomed knights.

1345-1450 Germ Warfare and the Black Death

For one hundred years the Black Death was the biggest news in Europe, but have you wondered how it got started in Europe? The Mongols somehow got the disease called Pasteurella Pestis. In about 1345, some Mongols were besieging the city of Kaffa on the Black Sea when the dreadful pestilence swept through their ranks. The Mongol commander got a great idea. He catapulted the diseased corpses over the city walls and the age of germ warfare began. From Kaffa, the Black Plague traveled to Mediterranean ports of southern Europe to Spain, France, Germany, and the British Isles, eventually killing almost half of Europe's population [over 25 million people]. This same disease brought an end to the Mongolian Empire as well.

1455-1560 Ottoman Empire

The Mongolians passed the Power onto the Moslems. The non-Mongolian Moslems took over much of the land left by the Mongols after their diseased finale. In addition to the Mongolian lands, they went on to gain much of the Mediterranean area.

27-Foot-Long Cannon-One of the reasons that the Moslems could take over so much land was a 27-foot-long cannon made by a Hungarian in 1452. Now you would think that this guy named "Urban" would be on the European side, which is correct, but the Byzantine emperor didn't want Urban's help so Urban decided he needed the money and helped the Ottomans. They got Urban's masterpiece; a cannon that had a 24-inch diameter barrel that hurled a 600-pound ball a range of over a mile. [**How would you like loading that round by hand?**] It was an almost unbelievable task just to position the huge thing. It took 30 wagons that were pulled and pushed by 60 oxen and 400 men, but it was worth it, because with it they conquered Constantinople and went on to conquer areas almost all the way around the Mediterranean Sea. [**For those who wondered, it was not a rapid-fire weapon.**]

Europeans Leave Europe-These Moslems seemed to be impossible to get rid of, so the Europeans looked outside of Europe for adventure and relief. We remember the initiator of this "Age of Discovery" as being Christopher Columbus, but he certainly was not. The real age of [re-discovery] probably happened immediately after the Aryan Wars and the Dark Ages that followed. These ancient explorers probably used maps from before the Tower of Babel incident and long-distance world trade became possible again. Some of the maps survived long enough to be copied onto other maps that were then copied on to other maps.

Reintroduced Maps

If people were in the wrong place during ancient times according to "Modern" historians, and that seems to be the case, how did they get there? The question might not be what mode of transportation, but rather how did they know where they were. Today we have more maps than we can possibly use as we try to find parts of the globe. After the Babel incident and the Aryan wars, the quantity of maps may also have been substantial. Man's wanderlust made it imperative to make new maps from the ancient maps. We know this because some of the copies of copies of copies have survived.

Knowledge of the World

Early man knew about the huge size of the Earth and that it was like a ball. By 240BC the Greeks had very accurately re-measured the earth to be 25 thousand miles in circumference, but well before that time, the bible and other early writings recorded the knowledge. Not only did ancient man somehow know about the roundness of the world; he, apparently, had similar language, similar writing, similar customs, and a similar basis for religion. Evidence has been found about their knowledge of the world. Maps have been found that show that early man had seen the entire world. There are even indications on some early maps that show Antarctica before the last plate shift, when Antarctica was not covered in ice. Written texts also tell us that everyone knew the world was a round ball.

Esdras II- Part of the Vulgate Bible, "Esdras II", speaks of a "round orb of the Earth."

Isaiah 40:22 *"It is he that sitteth **upon the circle of the Earth**, and the inhabitants thereof are as grasshoppers; that stretcheth out the heavens as a curtain, and spreadeth them out as a tent to dwell in."*

Asclepius- *In this historical work from the Nag Hammadi text it says: "These forces always are powerful **in the circle of the Earth**."*

France- *A multicolored, 6-inch diameter, globe that was made in 1531 shows the entire Americas as they were during prehistoric times. California is shown as an island instead of a peninsula as it is now.*

Popul Vuh- *Mayan history spoke of the great secret of human past, a long forgotten golden age when everything was possible. A time when men measured **the round face of the Earth and the 4 points of the arc of the sky**.*

Egyptian World Map

This Ancient Egyptian map showing that the world was round was made 5000 years ago. Notice the wings placed around the map, possibly, to indicate that the transportation method was by air. [See next left] I know this doesn't look like modern maps because it was a copy of a copy of a copy and finally copied by people that had no idea what it all meant. It possibly shows 2 factions of the earth and that the population or army size of the eastern group was greater than the western group.

 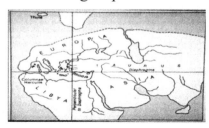

Dicaerchus Map

98

From Greece this map drawn by Dicaerchus about 300BC, shows many islands in the Mediterranean Sea that were not there even 5000 years before.

Crate Globe

This globe was made 150BC. Notice that Antarctica and the Americas were both shown during a time when neither was supposedly known about. [Left]

 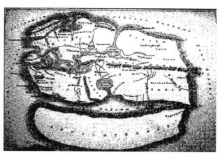

Mela Map

In 40 AD a map showing Antarctica was drawn by a Roman named Mela from more ancient maps. Supposedly, the Romans had no knowledge of Antarctica or the Eastern Asian coastline. [Above right]

Donnus Germanus Map

This Hemisphere map not only showed the knowledge that China was half way around the world, but it also shows knowledge of Antarctica.

Gloreanus Map

In 1510 this world map was drawn. The interesting part of this map is the knowledge of the American Pacific Coast. Have you heard anything about knowledge of the American West coast from data supplied in school? [Left]

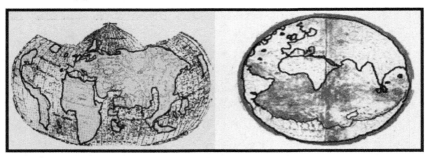

Lopa Hamen Map

In 1519, Antarctica was drawn as extending along the entire southern position as we know today. [Right]

Piri Reis Map

In 1511 an Arab named Reis was commissioned to make a map. It is believed that the map used as many as 20 source maps from map libraries in Constantinople which were destroyed during the 4th crusade. This took about 3 years and the Sultan was so pleased that he made Reis an admiral. [see following map]

He was not a good admiral and lost many ships and finally was beheaded, but the map remains and it has a peculiar nature. According to detailed studies by Charles Hapsgood, the map shows portions of Antarctica, the Falkland Islands, the Amazon river, and many things that no one knew about, or people didn't remember that we previously knew. Notice the large island near Florida where many artifacts from a sunken city have been found.

Does it Show Atlantis?

The map itself is loaded with notes to explain what was found around the world on different excursions. Mostly the explorers found naked people, but the two sites below had the notes shown. Both seem to be indications of the Atlantis Island from before the flood as both islands are no longer here. When the map of the world is placed over the Piri Reis map, the upper "Fish" picture is clearly shown where ancient historians claimed Atlantis to be.

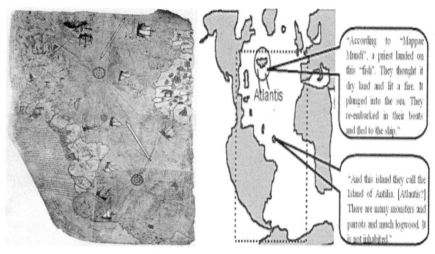

Oronteus Finaeus Map

Finaeus drew this map in 1531 showing Antarctica. The positioning is somewhat incorrect, but the most startling thing is that it shows rivers on Antarctica. Those rivers would not have been visible after the previous Earth shift in 8,000BC.

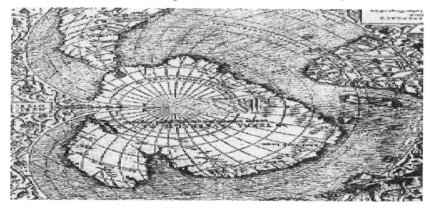

Hadji Ahmed Map

Redrawn in 1550, the Hadji Ahmed map shows a land bridge between Alaska and Siberia which hasn't been there since about 8,000BC.

Munster's Map

In 1550 this map was drawn which shows both coasts of the Americas, Hudson Bay, Alaska, the west coast of Russia, and Antarctica. Baja California is shown also as a long island. [See Next]

DeBry Map

In 1596 a man named Theodore DeBry showed the world with a huge continent of Antarctica-still undiscovered. [See next left]

Mercator Map

In 1569 a man named Mercator drew a map showing Antarctica's mountains and rivers which are now covered by ice. Possibly, the way it looked before the last major shift 10 thousand years ago. Of course, how did he know about Antarctica at all? [Above left]

Egyptian Map

In 1643 an Egyptian map was drawn possibly showing Antarctica as the central island between Africa and the Americas. This one has been used to show that Antarctica may have been the location of one of the "Atlantis" sites which Plato located in the "World Ocean as shown next left.

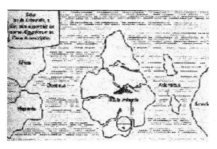 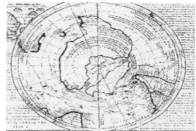

The Buache Map

Drawn in 1737, this map is unusual in that it fairly closely represents Antarctica as it is under the Ice and before the last shift about 7,000 BC. [Above right]

Pierre Mortimer Map

By 1700 the information about Antarctica seemed to have been forgotten, at least by most of the world as shown on the Mortimer world map.

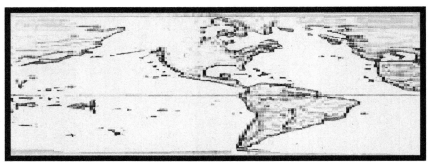

Many of the maps we have discovered appear to have been drawn from much earlier maps, showing that map making survived the worldwide flood, the Tower of Babel War, and the Aryan Invasions that followed, but map making wasn't the only thing to recognize. If you have maps, someone must have traveled to the places shown on the maps.

Re-re-discovered America

As I've stated many times now, "modern historians" love to eliminate uncomfortable aspects of our history. One such group of details that have been misplaced is the successful attempts at finding and colonizing the Americas. Recently some of them have surfaced, but it has been a struggle. Because of the difficulty people had throughout our recent history to recognize the continent of the Americas, they had to be rediscovered and rediscovered many times. After most of the flying ships discussed in book 3 had disappeared and after most of the ancient maps of the world had been lost, the new world had to be rediscovered by the people from the east and from the west. Although most of the voyagers and settlers will never be known, a tiny fraction of them left their mark on history. Here are some of the more widely known explorers and discoveries of the Americas. How many of the following can you recall from the "normal history" books? Columbus was one of the last to rediscover America. As you will probably notice, I feel that this whole reverence of Christopher Columbus is completely misplaced. The only thing that he should be known for is the initiation of female slave trade from the new world. We're going to see that many people from around the world discovered and explored the Americas well before old Chris.

Chinese in America

Chinese discovered America several times. The first time, as indicated in earlier chapters was before the flood, but the First in recorded time was about 2250BC. This was accomplished in the midst of one of the Dark Ages in our past.

2250BC-Chinese crossed the Pacific and return. They found the land of the strange face, where the sun rose. The recorded trip took 3 months to get to North America and another 3 months to get down to South America. The voyages were recorded in ancient texts.

2000 BC-*Petroglyphs were found and several studies were initiated in the area. One of interest was conducted in 1934 for the Pennsylvanian Historical Commission. From the study it was determined that the Iroquoian Indians of the area were invaders. On islands in the region several cultural layers was found in the ground, with the Iroquoia Indians on the top layer. The lowest was separated from the others by 8 feet of hard packed soil and estimated to be some 3 to 4 thousand years older. At this level was found 21 different groups of writings completely different than those of the natives above. Most of the writings were identified as Chinese based and included recognizable symbols for fortress, sun, water, heavy rain, prominent point, big and soil. Chinese had inhabited the East Coast of America long before most Europeans had thought about the new land. How they got there is somewhat of a mystery.*

500 AD-*Chinese send a Buddhist monk to the Americas and he returned after rediscovering America.*

On the following page is a picture of the voyage recorded in ancient Chinese texts. The wide band shows the current flow of the Pacific Ocean. According to the journal, the trip to the Americas took 90 days, while the equivalent trip from Europe took 80 days even though it was much closer. The Chinese didn't stop there. They traveled another 90 days and came to Ecuador or somewhere near there.

Phoenicians in America

106

Basque writing of ancient Phoenicians is distinctive and apparent. Although the first voyages were probably from North America to Phoenicia before the flood, no written record has been found of these early trips. A written legacy, however, has been found that shows Phoenicians traveled to the new world over 2600 years ago. By 40 AD the Phoenicians made it all the way to Ohio. Here are some of the writings found so far.

600BC, Pennsylvania, Phoenicians

Four hundred inscribed stones with Basque letters were found in 1940s. Here is an example. This type of writing was done in 600 BC.

Brazilian Phoenicians

In Brazil, the same writing has been found. Those Phoenicians went everywhere.

40AD Tennessee, Phoenicians

The Bat Creek Stone was found in 1889 by the Smithsonian Institute under one of 9 undisturbed skeletons, On the stone was Phoenician writings. Radio carbon dating showed a date of approximately 40 AD. Roughly translated it says *"--A comet for the Jews"*. [Left]

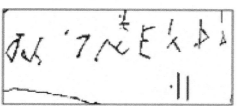 

0AD, Ohio , Libyan-Inscribed circular stone [coin like] found in 1890s written in ancient Libyan text. The translation is, *"The colonists pledge to redeem"* [Pervious right]

Arabs in America

The Arabs came to America over 2000 years ago. In Colorado, a billboard was made on a hill with a 4-foot stone heralding the prophet and the Koran form about 800AD. Probable translation, *"God is strong. Strong to help his right hand. The Koran? is the unique achievement of the prophet and tender." [Following right]*

0AD, Alabama, Arabs-An Iberic inscription on a stone was found. The translation is, *"A vegetable garden. Secession of land, a conveyance of property." [See previous left]*

Assyrians in America

Assyrians and Sumerians came to America possibly as early as 5 thousand years ago. It is called Fuente Magna, a strange statue found in Bolivia in 2002. It is not only extremely ancient, it contains SEMITIC and CUNEIFORM writings showing another example of a close communication between the Middle Eastern world and South America. The pictures following show the actual writings on the legs of this 6-foot-high statue.

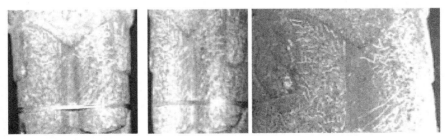

Translation of the texts is given below-*"Approach in the future one endowed with great protection the Great Nia".---"The Divine One Niash to Establish Purity, Establish Gladness, Establish Character". "This favorable oracle of the people to establish*

108

purity and to establish character for all who seek it".---"Use this talisman the Fuente bowl To sprout oh diviner the unique advise at the temple".---"The righteous shrine, anoint this shrine, anoint this shrine; The leader takes an oath to Establish purity, a favorable oracle and to Establish character. Oh leader of the cult. Open up a unique light for all, who wish for a noble life".

Another Assyrian Text-A cuneiform tablet from Assyria was found- on the banks of the Susquehanna River in 1921. The inscription described a loan to an Assyrian merchant in Cappadocia about 1800 BC.

Celts in America

Early Northern Europeans ventured over to the new world well before the time we usually think. As early as 0AD Celtic Ogham writings have been found as evidence of their travels and settlements. Even earlier evidence shows a long history of Celtic discovery.

1000BC Evidence-Fifty underground chambers mark the site of a Celtic community in the Hudson River Valley. The chambers are almost completely made of Quartz stone or granite which must have held some magical importance to the group. There are basically two types of chambers, cylindrical and oval. Many of the stones are massive and no mortar was required due to the fine working of the stones used in the construction. The newer of these structures was determined to have been built by the Druids by animal markings and runes identical with others found of the group around the world. This dates the later part of the community to about 3 thousand years ago and we can estimate the earlier settlement to be considerably older. Ancient Ogham writings have been found in the area which talk about praise for the spirit of nature during a high holy day. From these details it can be assumed that over **3000 years ago** the Celts established this settlement, well before Columbus. Even when the Druids reestablished the community, Columbus had not "Discovered" America.

800BC Ship-Ontario Rock carvings found show prehistoric ships identical to ship carvings in ancient Sweden.

0AD, Colorado, early Celts-Ogham writing and Egyptian like drawings were found on a stone. The translation indicated that the site was a Celtic ritual place. One of the figures inscribed looks like Anubis, one of the Egyptian gods. [See next left]

600AD W. Virginia, Celts-Ogham inscriptions were found on stones. The translation is "The reason of the blessed advent of the savior, Lord Christ, Salvatoris Domini Christi" This is believed to be the work of Irish Monks. [See previous right]

600AD, W. Virginia, Celts-An Ogham inscription was found. It is the longest known Ogham inscription in the world. A summary of the translation is *"—We insured they could not run away, but were unaware of the sounds of their approach, but made it to the cattle shelter. We passed in fear of bad tempered stampede of Bison that went into a narrow passage and over a cliff. Many clubs were used to finish them off."* [See below]

1171 AD **From Wales**

Prince Madoc found his way across the Atlantic, but he didn't write on any stones.

110

Norse in America

The Norse found their way to the Americas, but sometimes the quests were not successful. Sometimes the voyagers were killed by the natives, but they tried and they should be remembered for that.

1003 AD-The Viking Leif found North America.

1007 AD-The Viking Erickson found North America again. The map that follows shows the information that Leif Erickson brought back a thousand years ago. New-found-land can be clearly seen.

1355 AD-Norseman Paul Knutson found America again.

1362, Minnesota, Norse-In 1898, an inscription was found on a stone. The translation is, *"We were 8 Swedes and 22 Norwegians on a discovery voyage from Vineland. We anchored by 2 rocky islets, one day from this stone. We fished one day and came back to find 10 men dead. Ave Maria deliver us from evil. We have 10 men on the ship, 14 days from this island. Year 1362."* [Left below]

Jews in America

Jewish people or Jewish crossbreeds finally migrated to the new world. Some were here as early as 107BC, the problem is that they were in New Mexico and seemed to travel east. Certainly, they were here before 107BC, but the written testimony can be traced to that date. [See above right]

107BC, New Mexico, Hebrew-In the 1880s an inscription was found on an 80 ton stone, written in paelo-Hebrew letters and some Greek letters. Also, were found were many petroglyphs, one of which appears to be a star map depicted during a solar eclipse. This eclipse was determined to have occurred in 107BC. The translation appears to be an abridged version of the ten commandments. [See above right]

0AD, New Mexico, Hebrew-In 1860, a written text was found on a stone. It was inscribed in Hebrew letters. The translation is, *"Holy of Holies- King of the Earth- The Law of God- The Word of God"* [Below left]

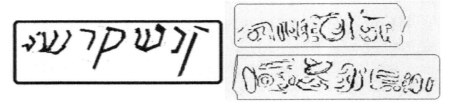

100AD, Pennsylvania, Hebrew-In 1864 through 1867, 5 stones were found. Each had written text inscribed in "a form of Hebrew". The letters on the lid and base were translated to say "Messiah". Other parts seemed to also be abridged portions of the ten commandments, just like the previous find. [See above right]

200AD Tennessee-Nine skeletons and this tablet were found together. The inscription reads. *"A comet for the Jews"*

Egyptians in America

Egyptians came over to America about 3000 years ago and colonized Arizona according to the written and physical evidence.

1000BC-The ruins of an entire 50,000 inhabitant cave dwelling community including Egyptian like hieroglyphics was found in 1906.

Mediterraneans in America

Ancient Italians and Greeks were not outdone. Writing analysis of a stone found in West Virginia indicates that they too had come to the Americas well over 2200 years ago. Within 200 years they were established in Michigan.

200BC, West Virginia, Iberian-In 1838, a sandstone disk was found with inscribed Punic letters. The translation is "the mound raised on high for Tasach---This title was given by his queen."

0AD, Michigan, Roman-A slate stone was found written in the time of Christ, pan-Mediterranean alphabet. The translation is *"I am carrying in accounts, 10 talents. To ten, 1 voided. I am collecting 11 only. Ten I can confirm. Transactions, 11 in all."* [Above right]

0AD-Runic script derived from ancient Greek was found on a stone in Colorado. It stated *"Here lies the servant of God Palladeis. I slew the slave of God."*

113

1121 AD- The Vatican commissioned Bishop Gnupsson to find the Americas, which, according to records; he did.

Americans Discover Europe

Some Americans went East and discovered the Old World.

*100AD-*A canoe with copper skinned sailors was found in Northern Europe. Naturally, the sailors were enslaved by the Romans.

Later Europeans Find America

The Mediterranean countries started reinvestigating the new world, even though they were a little late.

*1395AD-*The Zeno brothers from Venice found America. The Map that follows is one made by the Zeno Brothers. It clearly showing Greenland and a land mass beyond.

*1477AD-*A Portuguese navigator, "Coctereal", found America. He took the northern route like the Zeno's. [Knowledge of this trip probably gave Queen Isabella the confidence to support the Columbus voyage.]

*1492AD-*Christopher Columbus found the Caribbean for Portugal and took back his new commodity of slaves. We had better investigate this charlatan a little more and see if our children's text books are helping or hurting them.

1492AD Columbus & Syphilis

Columbus is known for a lot of things, but are they the right things? What we really know about him is that he was a fantastic liar, introduced young, Caribbean, slave girls as a money crop. He was also responsible for the new world's first "lost colony"; and more than likely, introduced syphilis to Europe. To top it off he was not a very good captain or navigator by all accounts, so why do we remember him at all? For proof we start over 2 thousand years ago.

Greek Navigation

In 240BC, a man named Eratosthenes was the head librarian at Alexandria. He decided that navigation to other places would be easier if navigators knew the distance around the earth. He rediscovered the circumference of the earth to be 25 thousand miles and also determined the earth's axis tilt to be 23 degrees before publishing the details in the book entitled "Geography". This work was the standard for many years and only very recently has our data been updated to have the earth's circumference at about 24,900 miles. Columbus and all the other navigators used this data and knew it to be correct for many years.

Columbus the Liar

No one wanted to fight the Moslems who were taking over the Mediterranean coastline, so people started to gain land other ways and the "new age of exploration" was born. No explorer is better known than Christopher Columbus, but there were several sailors trying to do the same thing as old Chris during this same time. Columbus was just the biggest liar. By manipulating known and calculated distances, he convinced Queen Isabella of Spain that the distance from Europe to "the Indies" was only 2500 miles and that it could easily be sailed to in less than two months. He knew it would take much longer, but he wanted the Queen's money. He also carried the lie much further by not letting his crew know what they were in for. He modified the ships books to keep his crew from knowing anything, so their trip was a complete horror, but it is apparent now that he probably knew all along how far he had to travel.

Isabella the Kind Hearted

Isabella had already had all types of fun by initiating the Spanish Inquisition in 1478 and by 1492, she had finally gotten rid of the 100 thousand pesky Jews that kept trying to stay in her country, so the Moslems took them in. [That doesn't happen too often today.] That same year, Christopher wanted to go find the land on the other side of the Atlantic and she had done everything else, so this was a natural. Other greedy sailors tried to gain their support in Spain, but had calculated distances of almost 10 thousand miles and the investors were not certain that the trip could be successful. Lying was the only solution.

No China Trip

Christopher's trip had nothing to do finding out if the earth was round nor did it have anything to do with going to the Orient. You may have been told these things, but they don't make sense. No "novice" navigator of the day would think that China could be so close and Christopher was no dummy. Just by measuring the time it would take a ship to disappear over the horizon would have allowed most, including Christopher, to know the approximate dimensions of the Earth and of course, Eratosthenes's very accurate measurements would have shown that trip to be over 10 thousand miles and impossible, except that most knew about the copper rich Americas and that is where he was going.

American Map

Not only had almost every navigator determined what the approximate diameter of the Earth really was, but also they had maps, by all accounts. Several maps of the world were still extant from ancient times, which showed the mid-ocean landmass that Christopher was after. We do need to know is that the distance from Europe to the "New World" is approximately 10 thousand miles and Christopher must have known it.

Columbus the Navigator

Speaking of lying; Chris's real name was Domenico Colombo, but the Christopher sort of stuck as a parallel to "Christ", I suppose, and he turned out to not be such a great sailor. In 4 voyages, he lost 9 ships. That was a terrible record. In fact, when he died, his funeral was not a lavish affair as other great navigators and explorers of the day. He was only a minor player by all accounts, but we praise him in every history book.

Domenico Colombo alias Christopher Columbus

No one knows what he looked like, but the previous drawing is the best guess we have from a number of descriptions.

Columbus the Slaver

So, what should Columbus be known for besides lying? In the early 16th century, Columbus tried to get to India, landed in America, and brought back his greatest discovery. He found that the young girl slaves didn't die as easily on the trip back to Europe as male slaves and they also brought the highest price. When he got back from his first trip, everyone was anxious for him to return and bring back more of this wonderful commodity. So, he went back and loaded up with more female prizes.

Columbus Found Syphilis

At the same time that the slave girls were introduced, syphilis, all of a sudden, came into existence in Europe and nobody knew where it came from. Evidently there was a substantial difference in the people of the two hemispheres and some diseases were more severe to the west and some were more severe to the Eastern populations of Europe. Syphilis was a terrible price for having American slave girls.

Columbus's Lost Colony

Not all of Columbus' men returned to bask in the glory of their new-found wealth and because of one such group Roanoke Virginia was not he first Lost Colony. On Chris's first trip, the Santa Maria was badly damaged and dismantled to make the first American fort/ village. With 40 "Volunteers" to protect the settlement, Columbus left for Europe with his syphilitic cargo. On his return, a year later, everything had vanished. From the generally friendly natives, the story was reconstructed. The "volunteers" thought that robbery and rape were OK with the friendly Indians. The Indians, over time, thought differently. Rape and pillage turned into retribution and revenge. Our other "first lost town" in Virginia probably had a similar cause, but somehow, we have glamorized and mystified its disappearance as well.

Columbus the Non-Slaver

Losing his fort was of little concern to Columbus on his return and he found that slaves weren't the only prizes to be found.

Unfortunately, the natives needed some incentive to help him in his venture. He designed a tribute system for the non-slave Tianos Indians that kept them from being slaves and made him a few bucks. There was gold in the ground, but Europeans didn't want to dig any gold for themselves, so the natives had to dig it up and give it to their "Master?"

Later this practice was augmented by the Spaniards. Every Taino over 14 years of age was to give a hawk's bell (about the size of a thimble) of gold to the Spanish, self-proclaimed rulers, every three months. Upon receipt of the gold, the natives were given tokens to wear around their necks as proof of payment. It was a simple system. When the Spaniards found Tainos without the appropriate tokens, they chopped their hands off, leaving them to bleed to death and making examples of them. It is estimated that about ten thousand Taino died handless that way. The engraving on the next page was from a 1598 engraving showing the brutality. Men and women both with hands cut off and bleeding to death almost like a sport. It might have been better to be a Spanish Slave than a free gold finder. That brings us to dogs.

Spanish Cannibals

Dogs are a man's best friend and it is no more obvious than those brought to investigate the new world. Unfortunately, no dog food was found in the new world, so natives were simply slaughtered to feed the dogs. The reason dogs were important is that during the investigations of the land, the dogs could easily keep up with the Spanish team and if no immediate food source was found, the dogs would be eaten as food. Just think about it. The human fed dogs, eventually, fed the humans. The Spanish were cannibals alright, just once removed.

Other Spanish Pleasures

The Spanish didn't simply kill for food either. Let's read what the Spanish missionary, Bartolome de las Casas, experienced. He saw, first-hand, how his countrymen terrorized the natives. This description is if of a single day, during which, the Spanish, evidently, dismembered, beheaded, or raped 3000 people.

"The Spanish cut off the legs of children who ran from them. They poured people full of boiling soap. They made bets as to who, with one sweep of his sword, could cut a person in half. They loosed dogs that 'devoured an Indian like a hog, at first sight, in less than a moment.' They used nursing infants for dog food."

Spanish Genocide

Using the European population density as a base, one estimate is that when Columbus did his "discovery" there were about 100 million "Indians" in the new world. These valiant, genocidic, hand chopping, dog feeding, slaving explorers were able to almost completely wipe out all of them within less than a hundred years. Why we get upset with Germans only genocidically killing 6 million and praise Columbus and those who followed him is beyond me. We even have a special day put aside as Columbus Day. I hope we don't come up with a Hitler Day.

Columbus the Stupid

There is one problem to my overview. The problem is that Columbus named the people of the Americas, Indians, supposedly because he truly believed that he was in the Indies. He may not have been all the bad things I said and only have been brain deficient. If that is the case, and he was stupid, I apologize. I'm just kidding. Columbus never thought he was in the Indies. The Indian name was a way to get more money for more trips. It is a travesty the way he and the rest of the "explorers" are treated in our history books. We feed this misinformation to our children without regard for truth and the 100 million or so people of the Americas are forgotten. The other thing that is generally forgotten is the "almost" Dark Age of 1492.

1490-1550 Almost Dark Ages

I'm tired of bashing Columbus and our teaching methods, so let's get back to meteors and in particular those that fell during Columbus's day. Fairly large meteors probably hit the earth just like those that had brought on the earlier Dark Ages, but the meteors weren't quite large enough to cause the sky to darken and the plants to all die. The meteors almost caused what I would call the Columbus Dark Age. Even after that more meteors fell and they also weren't quite large enough to initiate a Dark Age.

The "Age of Discovery" almost didn't happen.

We now believe that around 1490, in China a fairly large meteor fell from space, split into many pieces, and those pieces struck the earth. This event began an "almost Dark Age", which included destruction of parts of Europe and China. While a substantial amount of damage must have occurred, there is no significant information to suggest that the destruction was even close to that experienced during any of the real "Dark Ages". Read these two curiosities and see how close we probably were to another Dark Age. If this one is considered too small to count, we are due another at any time, so I'm counting it as a meteor strike.

*In China-According to Chinese traditional history, in about **1490** in China's Shanxi Province **tens of thousands** of people were killed by "falling stones".*

*In Germany-A German woodcutting from **1493** showed a huge "earthquake" probably brought on by the same event. It was of huge proportions with many totally collapsed buildings.*

More Meteors Fell

Since this "almost unfortunate time", other meteorites have frightened us. The one we typically remember is the one from 1908 which leveled a huge section of the Tunguska forest in Russia, but others, equally as spectacular, have been witnessed. Three other hits of similar size occurred.

One in Brazil in August 13, 1930. A huge ball of fire similar to the Tunguska event occurred.

A second one in Sikhote-Alin in February 12, 1947, was identified as multiple meteor strikes and substantial cratering.

In August 14, 1992 at least 48 meteors struck many roofs were damaged and one boy was struck in the head. Two months later a spectacular display is seen in Peekskill, New York as shown on the next page. One part hit a car and damaged it, but no one was hit.

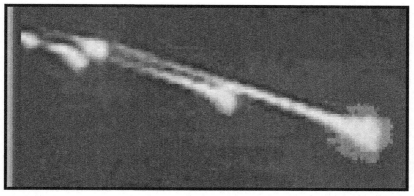

A 4th major event may have occurred in Greenland in 1997.

Isn't it strange that you were probably lead to believe that the meteor strike 65 million years ago was the last major strike on earth and you have no reason to believe that another would dare come close to us? Actually, there have been many major strikes and you have finally been introduced to them in this history. Speaking of history, let's see what the righteous Europeans were up to.

1560-1700 Europe

A caution about this section. It contains graphic violence and should not be read by the skwimish. I would suggest skipping this section, but it does show how low people had been driven during the age sometimes called renaissance. Spain, England and France controlled the world for a time. Everyone started discovering land. Not only did this notorious group control their own lands, but they believed it was **their duty** to take everyone else's land for the good of the infidels. "Investigators" were sent around the world to try to find new opportunities. If the current residents resisted, that was good too, because more slaves could be captured. What a great time. As I mentioned before, genocide was fine too. After all, the people in the Americas didn't know about Jesus. In Europe, two cousins did their part to destroy decency. Their names were Vlad Dracula and Erzabet Bathory.

I'll bet God really loved how the Europeans were spreading the Christian news to the world. The whole-scale genocide and cruelty has been downplayed to allow our heroes to shine and except for picking on poor Columbus, I'm not generally going to dwell on this time period but these ugly people were the rulers of Rumania and Transylvania. Many of you already know about them more because of the Dracula movies than history. These examples really show how bad people got when offered power as a ruler of a country during the age of enlightenment or renaissance.

Dracula the Impaler

In Rumania we find one of the most ruthless, and evil men known. His name was Prince Vlad III and he had a peculiar practice as punishment called impaling. During his younger life he often captured birds and mice which he proceeded to torture and mutilate. Some were beheaded or tarred-and-feathered and released Most were impaled on tiny spears. It was good practice for his later escapades. He actually was one of the Rumanian rulers during three different periods 1448, 1456–62, and 1476. You might have heard of his "sir" name [Dracula] or "from the house of the dragon". As the ruler his greatest pleasure was torture. Besides the normal torture type of thing, he placed long spikes outside his window on which victims were impaled. It is said that he would grease the poles and have the unfortunates try to hold on an adjacent shaft. Horses were tied to the victim legs and would pull the victim slowly down the shaft. As the grip failed, the body was shafted so to speak. To make his pleasure more refined, the end of the stake was usually oiled and care was taken that the stake not be too sharp; else the victim might die too rapidly from shock. Normally the stake was inserted into the body through the buttocks and was often forced through the body until it emerged from the mouth. However, there were many instances where victims were impaled through other bodily orifices or through the abdomen or chest. Infants were sometimes impaled on the stake forced through their mother's chests. The records indicate that victims were sometimes impaled so that they hung upside down on the stake. Death by impalement was slow and painful. Victims sometimes endured for hours or days. Dracula often had the stakes arranged in various geometric patterns. The most common pattern was a ring of concentric circles in the outskirts of a city that was his target. The height of the spear indicated the rank of the victim. The decaying corpses were often left up for months. It was once reported that an invading Turkish army turned back in fright when it encountered thousands of rotting corpses impaled on the banks of the Danube. In 1461 Mohammed II, the conqueror of Constantinople, a man not noted for his squeamishness, returned to Constantinople after being sickened by the sight of twenty thousand impaled corpses outside of Dracula's capital of Tirgoviste. The warrior sultan turned command of the campaign against Dracula over to subordinates and returned to Constantinople.

Thousands were often impaled at a single time. In 1459, on St. Bartholomew's Day, Dracula had thirty thousand of the merchants and boyars of the Transylvanian city of Brasov impaled. Impalement was Dracula's favorite but by no means his only method of torture. The list of tortures employed by this cruel prince reads like an inventory of Hell's tools: nails in heads, cutting off of limbs, blinding, strangulation, burning, cutting off of noses and ears, mutilation of sexual organs (especially in the case of women), scalping, skinning, exposure to the elements or to wild animals and boiling alive. Dracula's atrocities against his people were usually attempts to enforce his own moral code upon his county. He appears to have been particularly concerned with female chastity. Maidens who lost their virginity, adulterous wives and unchaste widows were all targets of Dracula's cruelty. Such women often had their sexual organs cut out or their breasts cut off. They were also often impaled through the vagina on red-hot stakes. One report tells of the execution of an unfaithful wife. Dracula had the woman's breasts cut off, then she was skinned and impaled in a square in Tirgoviste with her skin lying on a nearby table. Dracula also insisted that his people be honest and hardworking. Merchants who cheated their customers were likely to find themselves mounted on a stake beside common thieves. For a time, Vlad Dracula lost control of the land, but in 1476 he once again invaded his homeland. His small force consisted of a few loyal subjects, a contingent of Moldavians sent by his cousin Prince Stephen the Great of Moldavia, and a contingent of Transylvanians under their prince, Stephen Bathory [Remember the Name]. Dracula was again on the throne for a year. It ended with Dracula being buried alive. As far as we know he eventually died in his grave. If Vlad had the Dracula name, a certain countess in Transylvania had similar mannerisms. Her name was Erzabet Bathory. She was called the Blood Countess.

Blood Countess

Erzabet Bathory of Hungary was born in August 7, 1560. While Vlad usually is known as the real Dracula, there are problems with the thoughts. Vlad Dracula was Romanian and the storybook Dracula was Hungarian/Transylvanian like Erzabet. While he was blood thirsty, Vlad was never even rumored to have drunken human blood while Erzabet not only drank blood but was also reported to have bathed in the blood of virgins to keep her youth so let's investigate further. She was no match for Vlad when it comes to the thousands of victims he had, but she was no sloucher.

As a child Erzabet had witnessed the torture and execution of a gypsy, who was sewn up inside a horse and left to die there. This sewing thing was done by the "normal" people. As Erzabet grew she seemed to get enjoyment from unusual "punishment" things. Often she would stick "pins into the upper and lower lips of the girls or into the girls' flesh or under their fingernails". One particularly harsh "punishment" would be to drag girls out into the snow where she or her women servants poured cold water on them until they froze to death. On another occasion she demanded that one of her female servants be brought before her. Dorothea Szentes, one of Erzabet's "assistants, dragged one of Erzabet's servant girls to her bedside and held her there. Elizabeth rose up on her bed, and, like a bulldog, the Countess opened her mouth and bit the girl. The first bite reportedly was on the cheek; then she went for the girl's shoulders where she ripped out a piece of flesh with her teeth. After that, Elizabeth proceeded to bite holes in the girl's breasts.

She actually bathed in the blood of girls. Her many castles were equipped with chambers where she would hideously torture and mutilate her victims, becoming a murder factory where hundreds of girls were killed and processed for the ultimate, youth-giving ritual: the bath of blood or her frenzy for biting pieces of flesh off her victims. Most of her victims were peasants and no one cared, but when she ran out and started to go after aristocrats, she was stopped in her tracks. The trials were held in 1611. In the trial a list or register from the Countess's chest of drawers, put the number of girls killed at 650 and the list was in the proud Ladyship's own handwriting. Her several cohorts were found guilty of hideous crimes and sentenced to hideous death. The foremost perpetrators were sentenced to having all their fingers on their hands torn out by the public executioner with a pair of red-hot pincers; and after that their bodies should be thrown alive on the fire. A lesser accomplice was only decapitated. Erzebet, however, could not be found guilty, so she was walled up in a room and fed through a small hole until she finally died old and wrinkled without her rejuvenating blood.

In order to consider that they were enlightened, people of the time and even before this wonderful era found the real way to torture humanity. People found out that they could eliminate the precious past if they destroyed all the ancient literature.

Lost Libraries

We generally lie about our entire past, but that isn't the worst thing people of the past have done. Not only have we lied to ourselves and hidden information that doesn't go along with what we want to believe about the past; but also, we periodically destroyed information that could be useful and vital.

This "Age of Discovery" may have been the worst "Age of No Discovery" yet.

While people were re-writing history to make their version of history better, they were, at the same time, destroying ancient works that could jeopardized the "normal histories" that they had invented. We need to take a minute to mourn the loss of a substantial amount of scientific and historical knowledge. Many of the historical works were destroyed by overzealous leaders trying to either keep their people "safe" or other such nonsense. Imagine the information that we could have at this time if all the recorded documents were safe guarded and saved? They probably set back civilizations several thousand years. Here are a few of the many disasters that have jeopardized our technology and understanding. Just this list alone is staggering, and it is just the tip of the iceberg that greatly limited our development.

On the one hand, it seems that God didn't want us to know about everything and purposely kept information away from us to protect us, but the information is not what was bad, it was the mis-understanding of the information that continuously caused problems for mankind throughout the ages. Now that we have probably developed to a level that could use the information

129

appropriately, it is all gone. Maybe we are not ready and the destructions were by the "will of God", but I seriously doubt it. It still seems to be such a tragedy. Some of the destruction was well in the past, but--

---

--the "Age-of-Discovery" people did their part to ensure that their "interpretation" of religion, history, and science was not jeopardized.

Persepolis- *The library in Persepolis [ancient Persia] was destroyed by Alexander the Great. Hundreds of thousands of records, and books were gone in a flash.*

Alexandria- *The library at Alexandria in Egypt was destroyed by Julius Caesar. Some of the works were saved and sent to the Middle East, but most were destroyed. The estimated loss was over 700 thousand volumes. Remember that it took a long time to write a book in the old days, so almost all these works were non-fiction. By the way some of the text remained through several destruction periods, but the Christians destroyed the library again around 700AD.*

Memphis-[Memphis, Egypt that is]- *The temple of Ptah was totally destroyed along with its extensive library.*

Athens, Greece- *The famous collection of Psistratus was ravaged in 6th century BC.*

France- *The Bibracte Druid College was destroyed by the Roman conquerors. Thousands of documents were lost forever.*

Middle East- *The books that were sent to the Middle East from Alexandria were destroyed along with many more. Estimates of millions of books were used to heat the city bathhouses by the 3rd Caliph. The books warmth lasted 6 months according to historians.*

Carthage- *The library for Carthage and the Phoenicians was destroyed by the Romans in 146BC.*

Pergamom- *The library at Pergamom, in Asia Minor, supposedly housed 20,000 works—all gone.*

Byzantine- *Leo Isaurus burned an estimated 300 thousand works in Constantinople in the 8th century.*

Easter Island- *Almost all of the Rongo-Rongo tablets, the history of Easter Island, were burned and destroyed by well-meaning missionaries.*

Peru- *The 63rd ruler of the Inca "Pachacuti IV" destroyed the huge book known as the "Wisdom of Antiquity". We'll never know what marvels could have been discovered.*

China- *The libraries of China were decimated by Shih Huang Ti of the Chu Dynasty in 300BC. The books were burned by order of the emperor. Some protested and lost their heads.*

Now that most of the Ancient texts are gone, let's struggle on to the "Era of the American Colonies". Those times were not so great either.

17th Century American History

It is very easy to see that world history has been tainted by historians to bring out particular elements of the encounters of people around the world, up until the 16th century, but what about the history that Americans tell Americans. Surely that would be sacred to Americans. We'll start in the middle of the 17th century to confirm our dubious claims and take a look at the Pilgrims and the Puritans.

1637 Puritan Slavers

If we are going to address God loving European colonists, we need to address the Puritans. You remember them. They were the holier than thou guys. The Pequot Indians were an irritation to the Puritans, so they battled them, won and got some prizes; they took SLAVES. The ones they didn't keep, they sold to other Puritans buddies in Bermuda. After the slaving, they went back to their prayers.

1620 Pilgrim Pirates

Here is where the disease problem went the other way from that of Columbus's Syphilis. This is a more accurate, but less awe-inspiring account of the Plymouth Rock incident. For some reason, the story has changed over the years to make the Pilgrims seem like heroes, but that is not the way the evidence bends. In the Early 17th century, instigators aboard the Mayflower, pirated the ship and forced the captain to veer away from Virginia and head to what is now Massachusetts so that they wouldn't have to conform to the religious and social requirements of the Virginian region. In school, our modified history books try to indicate that the experienced captain could somehow get off course by hundreds of miles and if that were possible, he didn't try to go back to civilization in Virginia once he got his heading. Yeah right!

Accidentally Landing in Tecumseh's Home-The pirates had an American Indian "servant" named Tecumseh with them. He promised them his help in return for going home. Isn't it strange that the Mayflower accidentally came ashore where Tecumseh lived? These people knew exactly what they wanted to do and probably had planned it from the beginning.

Pilgrim Grave Robbers-Whenever they got to their accidental destination, the pilgrim pirates had almost nothing. They would have died during that first winter except for one thing. That was the Bubonic Plague. Again, our historians lack absolute truth in their descriptions.

Several years before, other American settlers had brought with them several things, but among them was a disease which killed an estimated 80 to 90 percent of the East Coast American Indians including almost all of the tribe from which Tecumseh had come. The remaining Indians fled as fast as they could to get away from the terror. The dead remained in the village where they died. Blankets, clothing, food, shelter, and everything that the new settlers would need to survive a winter stayed with the dead Indians. The pilgrims were desperate, so they stole everything from these open-air graves and Tecumseh had no choice but to help them through the first winter or die himself. This story sounds a little different than the one in what I loosely term as our "History Books", but which story do you believe? Were the Pilgrims accidental heroes or calculating pirates who robbed the graves of the dead to survive a torturous winter? Don't answer right now. Let's go to the 18th century.

18th Century America

I'm not going to dwell on historical items you can get from another book, but I do think there are some elements in the 18th century that should be recognized. The 18th century was no better when it comes to reporting an accurate history. For one thing, we can't even tell our children who their presidents were because we are afraid to confuse them. Being ignorant of the facts may make us less confused, but it is still a terrible thing. Presidents and submarines are not the only confusion in our history during this time. We also mix up capabilities of our heroes like Ben Franklin and ignore strife like our first "almost Civil War. I know the American Revolution was fought during this time period, but most have already heard about that war; except for the submarines and the requirement for running, so I thought I should at least, bring out those subjects to broaden our perception.

Boston Tea Party Misconception

We have all heard about the Boston Tea Party, but students are continuously misinformed about one of the key initiators of what has been called the American Revolution. The Boston tea party did not happen because the British raised the price of tea, but because they lowered the price of tea. This made a few influential colonialists mad. Here is the real story.-----Such a huge black market existed in the colonies, that a cheaper British tea threatened to make the smuggling of tea unprofitable. Angered, not only by the loss of the tea trade but also by the monopolistic practice of the British East India Trade Co., colonial black-market smugglers joined the radicals agitating for independence. If it wasn't for the support of these black market "traders", the radicals

134

may not have been able to start the war. That doesn't sound as nice as fighting against "Taxation without Representation" so the truth is hidden. Another truth that should be brought out is that the revolution was NOT a revolution, but we'll talk about that a little later. Right now, let's go under water.

Submarines & the Supposed Revolution

If you are talking about under water, submarines come to mind. The submarine we need to look at is one that helped us win the War. Submarine warfare in the 18th century is not widely discussed and generally classified as insignificant, but I don't think it was. The year was 1776 and the submarine's name was the Turtle. A drawing of this craft is shown below left. On the night of September 7, 1776, the Turtle, operated by Sergeant Ezra Lee, conducted an attack on the British ship HMS Eagle. A boring device that was operated from inside the Turtle was used, but it failed to penetrate the target vessel's hull. The Turtle's torpedo, a keg of powder, was to be attached to an enemy ship's hull and detonated by a time fuse. Although the torpedo was never attached to the target, the clockwork timer detonated it about an hour after it was released. The result was a spectacular explosion that ultimately forced the British to increase their vigilance and to move their ship's anchorage further out in the harbor. This, of course cost the British much needed time and manpower to adjust their docking and security, which may have greatly aided in our victory.

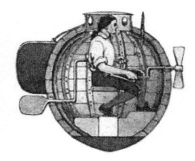

135

Previous Submarines

That wasn't the first time the British had known about submarines, so they knew that a submarine could have been made that could do great damage to their fleet. In 1620 a Dutch inventor named Drebbel designed a submarine that was propelled by 12 rowers as depicted above right. King James I of England reportedly took a ride in the strange craft down the Thames River as it traveled 15 feet below the surface. This predecessor was not used in war, but blowing up the ships as they arrived on colonial soil was a fantastic plan, because both sides used muskets and that was a terrible way to fight a war.

The Musket & the Revolution

Have you been told that the Americans won the "Revolutionary War" partially because the British soldiers were so stupid that they fought in a straight line and the Americans played a cat and mouse game to attack the enemy by surprise?

That hide-and-seek war never happened and you have been fooled again.

The major weapon of the revolutionary war was the musket and it used black powder. Black powder builds up in the barrel very quickly so the bullet used was much, much smaller than the barrel or it would get stuck. When it left the end of the barrel as it rattled its way down the barrel, no one could determine where the bullet would go. Sometimes it went left. Sometimes it went up. Almost never did it go where you wanted it to go. In fact, there were no sights on the muskets, because they would have been useless. Firing from a secured site like behind a tree would also have been useless, because once you position is known, someone would come over and kill you while you were reloading. The only way musket wars could be fought was by having a long line of men fire at the same time. With enough bullets whizzing around, some of the enemy would go down if they were close enough. When I

136

say close I mean less than 50 yards from one another. The old saying, "Wait until you see the whites of their eyes", wasn't just an emblem of courage, it was a strict necessity for two reasons. First was the inability to hit anything, but another more important reason was what you could call "run time" and this is another concept that has not made its way to our history books—possibly because it would show that the British were NOT the boobs presented in American histories.

The Running War

The bullet firing from a musket was really only used to disrupt the enemy's line so that the real weapon could be used-----the bayonet. The soldier would wait as long as he could and then fire his musket. Hopefully the enemy would have some holes in his "line" but the enemy would fire anyway. If the enemy fired, the attacker had less than 20 seconds before the enemy could reset the line, reload a new round, and fire. Running towards the enemy as fast as the soldiers could go, the soon to be winners would breach the hole and start stabbing. Now that's a war of bravery. Hiding behind a tree and then jumping out to fire your musket was useless, dangerous and fatal. You didn't need sneaky soldiers. You needed fast runners and sharp bayonets.

Civil War Enhancements

It should be noted that during the Civil War of 1861 [our 5th Civil War], weapons were about the same, except that bullets were made closer to the size of the barrel so the bullet would go farther and straighter. Therefore, opposing teams could get farther from each other. You guessed it; often, bullets would stick in the barrel and a soldier would be in a major dilemma. After the battle of Gettysburg, for instance, many rifles were found with rounds still plugging the barrel. One discarded weapon was noted to have 26 ammunition loads, each packed-on top of a previous one in the barrel. The unfortunate soldier had desperately tried to fire his clogged weapon over and over, but he never hit anyone.

We'll discuss misconceptions about the Civil War a little later. Right now, we need to get back to the Revolution as colonialists prepare to fight on Bunker Hill.

The Battle of Bunker Hill Never Happened

The colonials were supposed to dig in on Bunker Hill, but for some reason they chose Breeds Hill instead. It was a smaller hill about ½ mile away. The rest of what you have been taught seems to be correct. The British and American Colonial Tories succeeded in taking this "WORNG" hill, but they lost over 1000 men doing it. The colonial rebels only lost about 400 men. The reason I brought this up is that it is a good example of what historians typically do with their mistakes. Later "to avoid confusion", the people trying to protect our "made up" history renamed Breeds Hill and now Breed's Hill is Bunker Hill so history is again correct. --- I don't know how they changed the name of the real Bunker Hill, so don't ask me..

1765-1789 Who was Running America?

Our First Presidents

Everyone knows that Washington became President in 1789 so the question might be, *"Who ran the country after the first declaration of Independence until George Washington took over in 1789?"* Here is still another example how history gets twisted. We signed our country into our first Civil War with the 2nd Declaration of Independence in 1776 and the Revolutionary War was over in 1780, but something is wrong with what we are taught in school. Didn't we have a president during the time between the time of the Declaration that made our country a sovereign entity and George Washington's reign in 1789? The answer is we had many Presidents before Washington and John Hancock can be thought of as our "real" first President [*after our 2nd Declaration of Independence and our 2nd Constitution*]. George was our 13th president after the separatist rebels pushed the United States towards independence from England with a second Declaration of Independence. He could be considered the 8th from the end of the Revolutionary War so you can take your pick, but don't simply pick number one. George's only "first of a kind" distinction was that he was the first after we changed our constitution from the one we called the "Articles of Confederation", to the one we call simply the "Constitution" today. That doesn't mean we should simply forget the other Presidents does it? After all, George wasn't even elected like we think of elections today. There was no opposing party, so, guess what; he was voted in unanimously. I know that doesn't sound like the American way, but it worked for George. John Adams was the 1ˢᵗ President elected by the People. The first 12 Presidents in order are very briefly described below. I don't want to belabor this historical travesty, but I think we should at least recognize them as brave and important men of American history.

Before the First President

As I mentioned the 1ˢᵗ Declaration of Independence was in 1767 and the following Presidents ruled over our governing body; Timothy Riggles, Peyton Randolph, and Henry Middleton Their pictures are shown below. Many do not include Timothy Riggles as he was the first traitor President and became a commander of an English troop during our 1ˢᵗ Civil War.

The New 1ˢᵗ President

If you have wondered why John Hancock was the only signer of the Declaration of Independence on its day of release, the answer is simple. John Hancock was President of the United States at that time. He served between May1775-Oct. 1777. He only left because his gout was getting unbearable. His most remembered action was being President during the first American Civil War that started on July 2, 1776. Some may know it as the Revolutionary War, but you will see it was certainly a Civil War fought over inappropriate taxation just like the other 4 Civil Wars. Oh, yes! You thought it was July 5ᵗʰ didn't you. The declaration was initiated on the 2ⁿᵈ and the war had begun; more about that a little later. Finally, President Hancock signed the 2ⁿᵈ Declaration on the 4th and none of the other "patriots" signed the document for months or even years. The Americans were in the midst of their first civil war, but the British would not know it for another two weeks. The country kept on running as usual, but some of the Americans began fighting each other in a more organized fashion. [Hancock, the Pirate President is shown next left] Let me tell you something special about this President. He was the richest President until President Trump in 2016 and he was the 49th richest American before 2003 with a net worth of about $800 million in 2003 corrected dollars.

2nd President

Henry Laurens was President from November 1777 until December 1778. After his term, he still was trying to make our nation great. In 1780, he went to solicit a loan from Holland and to negotiate a treaty; but on his passage, he was captured by the British. After being sent to England, he was committed to the Tower, as a State prisoner, on a charge of high-treason. Here he was confined more than a year, and was treated with great severity. Henry Laurens was a great American, a war hero, and President. [See our first prisoner of war President above middle]

3rd President

John Jay was President from December 1778 until September. 1779. He had refused to sign the Declaration of Independence, so you would think that this position was not warranted, but John Jay actively tried to build our nation and by the time Washington came along he was elected as the first Chief Justice of the Supreme Court, so don't worry about his loyalty. [See our first President to believe his Chief Justice seat was more important above right]

141

4th President

Samuel Huntington was President from September 1779 until February 1781. The war was waging and his main job was trying to scurry up supplies for the troops. That was not simple task as there was no money to scurry up. In February, his health became so bad that he had to resign, but he, like the others, should not be forgotten. If Samuel Huntington hadn't been so forceful in trying to get our troops clothing and supplies, he might have not gotten so sick, but the war might have been lost. Let's not forget our 4th president as he had been an indentured slave who work hard to become one of the premier lawyers of his day. [See our first Slave President next left]

5th President

Thomas McKean was President from February 1781 until November 1781. He was commissioned a colonel in the New Jersey militia and served as President of the newly independent Delaware. In 1777, still serving in the Congress under the Articles of Confederation, he was appointed Chief Justice of Pennsylvania, an office that he held for nearly twenty years. He was elected President of Congress in 1781. I know we were still at war with the British but our country had a President just the same. [His image is shown previous right]

6th President of the United States

John Hanson was President from November 1781 until November 1782. Many times, he is considered the 1st as well. He certainly was 1ˢᵗ president after the 1ˢᵗ Civil War ended and he was unanimously elected. Again, his major problem was trying to pay the troops of the war now called the "American Revolution", but by this time, the Continental Currency was almost worthless. He also ordered all foreign troops off American soil, as well as the removal of all foreign flags. There could be no question that President Hanson ruled our Country courageously and effectively. Some will say that the United States was not a true nation until the adoption of its first Constitution, called "The Articles of Confederation", which was adopted on March 1, 1781. That also makes Hanson our 1ˢᵗ President. If that is so, I think there are many NON-COUNTRIES around today. No matter what your feelings are on this, the 1ˢᵗ constitution document was proposed on June 11, 1776, but not agreed upon by Congress until November 15, 1777. Maryland refused to sign this document until Virginia and New York ceded their western lands. "Here is a funny part. Maryland was afraid that these States would gain too much power in the new government from the huge land masses. Later we find the exact opposite occurs and the large States all loose representation power to tiny States like New Hampshire. [Our first President After the War Ended is below left]

Another John Hanson

As a note, there has been some confusion about two John Hansons. The one pictured to the right above was not a President of the United States but was, instead a senator in Liberia in the 1850s. I know that both have the same name and there is a family

143

resemblance, but do not mistake the two even though some Internet sites try to say this black man was the 6th President simply because his name was the same. The Information is false.

7th US President of the United States

Elias Boudinot was President from November 1782 until November 1783. He is also considered the 1st President. As President of the Continental Congress, he signed the Treaty of Paris, and was for a time called President of the United States in Congress Assembled. After his Presidency, he was appointed first director of the United States Mint. [See below left]

8th US President of the United States

Thomas Mifflin was president from November 1783 until November 1784. During his term, a ban of slavery was narrowly defeated. Wouldn't that have changed things? As the first President to try to abolish slavery, he should certainly be remembered more than Lincoln. As we find out later, Lincoln's selfish desire to bring out black America problems, was not to help that segment of America, but, instead was done for a less than honorable reason. Thomas Mifflin, on the other hand, was an honorable 8th President. [Preceding middle]

9th US President

Richard Henry Lee was President from November 1784 until November 1785. He was one of the Declaration of Independence signers who won the presidential election. As a funny note, he ran under the Anti-Administration Party. [See above right]

10th US President

John Hancock [below left] was President for a second term from November 1785 until November 1786. Many loved him, but when he was elected, he was too sick to really perform his duties. During his entire term, David Ramsay and Nathan Gorham shared his duties. John Hancock was too sick to even resign during the end so his reign continued the entire year. Ramsey and Gorman were the real Presidents.

David Ramsay to the left was, essentially, President first ½ of Hancock's reign. [Middle]

Nathan Gorham on the right was, essentially, President second ½ of Hancock's reign. They, too, should not be forgotten.

11th US President Arthur St. Clair

This man was born in Scotland instead of one of the colonies. Although he wasn't born in the United States, Arthur St. Clair became President from February 1786 until November 1787. During his term, the most notable event was the end of the second Civil War simply called the Shay's Rebellion. After he left the Presidency, he became governor of the vast Northwest Territory and led 2 major defeats of the white-man against the overpowering Indians. [Below left]

12th US President

Cyrus Griffin was President just before Washington. [January 1788- November 1788 His most notable action, was the transition from a country operating under the Articles of Confederation to one operating under its 2nd Constitution simply named "The Constitution"? [Above right]

These are the forgotten Presidents. Please remember these American Heroes. By the way, are you wondering why we don't we talk about them?

Here's the Problem

The reason we don't talk about the first 12 presidents is that America had troubles with our first constitution. So, we started over counting presidents when we changed to a "Constitution" that emphatically Stated that ALL RIGHTS **NOT** EXPRESSLY GIVEN to the federal government will be given to the States. I know that there has been some confusion about our first Presidents, so I thought that I should clear up some of this confusion.

List of 1st Presidents

Timothy Riggles was first President after the 1st Declaration of Independence.

Peyton Randolph was 1st President after the 1st Constitution

Samuel Huntington was 1st President After the 2nd Constitution

John Hancock was first President during the first part of the Revolution and was the only signer of the Declaration of Independence on the first day of its issuance, so he is called the first President.

John Hanson was the first President after we won the Revolutionary War.

Elias Boudinot was considered the 1st President because he was the first President to sign the Treaty of Paris which marked the end of the Revolutionary War.

I'm not exactly sure why George Washington is sometimes called the 1st president except that he was the first president after our third Constitution was adopted.

I suppose we could go farther and call John Adams the first President as he was the 1st to actually be elected by a general population.

Take your pick, but don't forget these great American Presidents that molded our nation for the good or the bad. That brings us to the 2nd Civil War.

Here's the Problem

The reason we don't talk about the first 12 presidents is that America had troubles with our first constitution. So, we started over counting presidents when we changed to a "Constitution" that emphatically stated that ALL RIGHTS **NOT** EXPESSLY GIVEN to the federal government will be given to the States. Everyone liked the words of this Constitution for a while.

People Forgot the Constitution

I am not necessarily a strong constitutionalist, but it has become painfully obvious to me and most other people that our current government has thrown out that basic requirement and now uses an "Unwritten Constitution" which says the exact opposite to the "Real Constitution". This new one is believed to say, "Any rights

147

not expressly given to the States will be **taken** by the Federal government." Maybe we should start numbering the presidents over again with this new constitutional idea. Maybe Franklin D. Roosevelt was our first president with the big Federal government concept or maybe we should have restarted when President Grant tried to rid us of our constitution. It's not fair to John Hanson and the others to not start over. Another thing that is just not right is how we present our 5 Civil Wars to our children. It is a total crime.

America's Five Civil Wars

The Civil War we usually here about is only one of at least 5 uprisings, which threatened to break up the United States. The 5th was the bloodiest, but the others were not insignificant. Here is an overview of the causes and outcomes that you may never have heard previously. The first was the one we mistakenly call the American Revolution.

Tea-Tax Civil War of 1776

As I mentioned previously, there have been some misconceptions about this war. Let me continue with several "mistakes" that are usually provided as fact concerning this first American Civil War. The colonial government had been squabbling among themselves and on July 2 1776, war was declared. The war to follow would, generally, be between the rebel colonialists [Mostly merchants that made up about 1/3 of the population who didn't like England having controls over the pricing of their goods] and the Torie colonialists [British rule supporters who made up about 1/3 of the United States population at that time] not the British government against a unified group of people who tried to overthrow the British government. Very few non-Americans were killed in the war, but many American colonialists died in this first of many Civil Wars. We believe that about 5 thousand rebel Americans dies and about 4 thousand Torie Americans died in the war. A couple of thousand others died, but don't let anyone tell you that it wasn't a civil war. Everyone knows that a Revolution is where a significant group of country rises up and takes over a country. The truth is this. No one took over England and most of the people fighting in the "civil" war were Americans so let's not kid ourselves. This was the first American Civil War. If you notice, I indicated that it started on July 2nd not the 4th as you probably were told. The Congress entered into the war on the 2nd of July. Why we celebrate the 4th is beyond me except that the American president, John Hancock, and his secretary signed the proclamation document on the 4th. That makes no sense either in that most of the other representatives of the congress didn't sign the document for almost a year so no one would use the signing date for a major holiday. Besides the wrong timing we have the "liberty Bell". Possibly bells rang to celebrate the beginning of the war during the month of July, but the Philadelphia "liberty bell" was most likely not one of them The Liberty inscription had nothing to do with this Civil War, but instead, it represented freedom from the insanity of slavery. Speaking of freed slaves, torries and freed slaves left by the thousands during and after the war. Most resettled in Canada with the help of the British government.

Shay's Farm-Tax Civil War of 1786

Even after the first war was won by the rebels, our Nation wasn't too stable and something called "Shay's Farm-Tax Rebellion" occurred during President St. Clair's term. The poor farmers in western Massachusetts and the surrounding area had just about enough of the industrial States. Unequal taxation with respect to cost of goods sold put a heavy burden on the farmers. Soon their lands were in foreclosure. In desperation, some decided to form a rebellion of secession. Of the three major battles, the most notable was made up of 2000 Agrarian soldiers against 1600 Union Soldiers.

The Union side won and the nation stayed together with the miniature States [that I call the Statettes] like Vermont, New Hampshire, Rhode Island, Connecticut, and New Jersey all gaining more power. This will become an important problem later.

Whiskey-Tax Civil War of 1794

Nothing really changed from the preceding uprising, so another one soon followed. Like its predecessor the third one was due to concentration of power in the industrial States at the expense of the farm States. The cause of the third Civil War is more insidious and even less discussed than Shay's War. Here is a brief overview. Because of inappropriate land taxation, an unusual requirement to force all legal proceedings in the "east" and a 28% tax on the production of whiskey, money from western Pennsylvania, Virginia, and other areas had become nearly worthless. Influential "eastern industrialists" bought the worthless currency and land deeds attached to debt at pennies on the dollar and the government then purchased the **21 million dollars** from the "fortunate investors". Here is the sneaky part. After the money was in the hands of the few influential "friends of the right people", the government bought the almost worthless money at face value, which in turn greatly increased the value of the now easterner-owned land. The westerners were desperate before the mysterious generosity of the United States Government and now they were more desperate. I know to some this coincidence might seem odd as it did to the "westerners" who finally revolted. The most significant war event included about 6 thousand western farmers against 13 thousand Union soldiers. The agrarians lost in every way, but the loss of life during this Civil War was less than 100 men total. Their spirits were broken and the Statettes gained more power.

The Almost Civil War of 1806

Louisiana-Purchase [almost] Civil War -The major cause of this almost insurrection was the Louisiana Purchase, but it really started back in 1763 when France ceded the territory known as Louisiana to Spain. The community flourished, but in 1800 Napoleon demanded it back. Spain complied on the condition that the territory would not be sold. Napoleon agreed and immediately sold it to Jefferson. Here's where the real problem occurred. The new United States owners disregarded property ownership of the people there and provided almost no protection to the citizens. They were simply miserable.

That was about the time that Hamilton was shot by Aaron Burr [shown on the left] who reportedly was to be the next Emperor of the "Western Territory' when and if Louisiana and several of the western States separated from the union. Although Burr had lost the New York Governor race and publicly blamed his loss on Hamilton, it is believed that another possible reason for Burr's fight was Hamilton's refusal concerning his joining the insurrection. The reasons were lost in history and Hamilton was dead. Emperor Burr had two other major players that had joined him. These included Generals William Eaton and James Wilkinson. At the time, Wilkinson, was commander of all United States military forces in the West, so this was going to be a significant war.

Evidently, Eaton was captured and informed the right people of the insurrection before the war could begin. No battles were fought except for the Hamilton duel. After the capture of the Emperor and the Generals, the secession plans were squelched and misery in the land of Louisiana continued. Mr. Burr was acquitted due to lack of evidence and fled to Europe.

Probably the War of 1812 really stopped the almost 4th Civil War from getting much steam, because people started to have money

152

and people with money are happy people. Tensions didn't get bad for another 35 years because people found a new way to distract themselves from the tension of the growing nation. We'll look at that story in a minute, but let's first look gold. While all the wars were going on, gold was becoming a great distraction in 19th Century America. There were two things that were really important in the 19th century and they were not the Civil War and slave freedom. The important driving elements of this time were the railroads and GOLD. You might not have heard the whole truth about these events.

19th Century America

You're not going to believe this but the 19th century was not reported correctly. Let me first look at the issue of killing for gold. During the 19th century, the historians not only let racial sensitivity cloud the events, but America as a whole made inappropriate compensations for both black and red skinned Americans to ease our minds. One reason the people of the United States felt bad about red skinned Americans was gold in Georgia. As it turned out gold wasn't the only reason to push the red skinned Americans around, but it was one of the first really bad ones.

1828-1861 Gold

First there was the Georgian Gold Rush of 1828. The biggest thing about this gold rush besides the 300 ounces a day gold finds was that the Cherokee Indians were yanked from their land so that the "Americans" could get rich. About 1849 the mines began to play out and the Cherokees had all been moved away but most of them didn't want to go. Still people wanted more gold. Not to worry, here comes the Californian Gold rush of 1848. Then, in 1851, the Australian Gold rush came along followed by the New Zealand Gold Rush in 1861. In 1896 the people had to come back to Alaska where more of the golden metal was found. People were jumping, taking boats, living in mountains and dying. Very few made enough to survive and "get rich quick" turned into "working continuously, becoming a pauper, and dying quickly". This section of our history is typically glossed over because we didn't have strong heroes and national secrets to protect, but it was also a sad time as hope quickly turned into desperation and destitution. From this destitution came alcoholism and from that we got something called a wake.

Lead and Whiskey Wake

Today, we hold a "wake" for the dead and it was very popular in the 19th century, but why? No one seems to tell you. They just say it is a custom. One answer for the "Custom" is **lead and whiskey**. People would drink whiskey out of lead cups in the old days. The Whiskey would cause the lead to leach into the drink and be swallowed. Sometimes people would be knocked out for days as the lead rotted the brain and the "wakey" would be laid on a table for a couple of days to see if he was really dead. Soon, it would be obvious if he was going to recover or if his lead cup should be given to another.

15th Century Wake-Before the common use of lead or getting that drunk, the "wake" custom of the 15th century had to do more with evil spirits. Once it was known that the spirit had left the body, the dead body could be buried, his family would keep vigil for a couple of days just to make sure no bad guys got their loved one's spirit. In a few days the spirit was known to have left and burials were safe; at least burying them was sort of safe.

Saved by the Bell -Let me digress for a minute more while we are on the subject of burying the dead. Several hundred years ago, in England they ran out of places to bury dead people, so they began the quaint custom of pulling up coffins, pouring out the bones, and putting another corpse in its place. They found that 1 out of 25 coffins contained scratch marks, so the "wake thing" was pretty important in my estimation. People got so scared about this finding that they attached bells to strings that traveled to the coffins. If one woke up in a coffin, he would only have to ring the bell and others would uncover him, or at least that is the theory. The almost dead guy was considered to be "saved by the bell" if someone yanked him out of his hole so we use the expression today any time we are given a bell to ring from our coffins. I know that being "saved by the bell" also could mean that children didn't have to answer questions because the end-of-class bell rang, but this history is more colorful so I'm sticking with it.

John Quincy Adams & Andrew Jackson

While all this gold rushing, lead drinking, and body waking was going on, we had an election that was peculiar. It was 1824, and for this particular presidential election there were 4 popular candidates, each from the same party, because we still only had one party. All that seems unusual, but "ok" except what happened next wasn't so "ok". Andrew Jackson won by a landslide, gaining **33% MORE** votes than his next rival, John Quincy Adams, but because he didn't have quite enough "electoral" votes to be considered a majority, Congress got into the picture. In a back-room deal, one of the other candidates, Henry Clay, was given the opportunity to change from losing Presidential candidate to winning Vice Presidential candidate to put John Q. over the top.

Six More Presidents Won Against By Electoral Vote- Americans were soon to find that the massive urbanization of a very few cities became a hugely powerful controller for the entire country. After all they had more individuals. Why should North Dakota count anyway? The Electoral college would help control the massive urban sites by spreading the voting to regions, All about the same size, the voting issues associated with the tiny Statettes was neutralized and the entire country had a say in the elections. While most elections were still in line with the "popular" vote, 6 stand out showing how important the Electoral College really is.

Lincoln, Harrison, Hayes, Nixon, GW Bush, and D. Trump.

John Tried to Change the Constitution-Once John Q. was in office, he tried to change the government into a federally controlled nightmare. He came up with horrible things like the following:

Federal control and support for literature,
Federal control and support for art,
Federal control and support for universities,
Federal control and support for science expeditions,

He tried other similar things that were totally against the Constitution as well. Usually his mistakes are not highlighted in our schools today, probably because we are USED to presidents and congress violating the Constitution. This was not the case in the 1840s and 50s. He was out of office as soon as the people found out what kind of a "Constitution violator" he really was and the "Constitution acceptor and States Rights advocate", Jackson, took his place, like he should have from the start. We will be looking at this Constitution again a little later. First let's skip ahead to 1850 to look at the steps that lead up to the 4th and 5th Civil Wars. There seemed to be fairly low tension until this time. Then we experience a major fiasco.

The California Fiasco

When I say fiasco, I mean in terms of the Farming States. In 1818 there was enacted a law which forced introduction of States to both the "Agrarian or slave state" side and the "Industrialist or quasi-non-slave state" side at the same frequency. The law used something called the Mason Dixon line to separate the two groups and for several years it had insured a relatively equal split in the congressional voting. The Farm States had a voice and the Industrialists had a voice. For each new state above the line coming in as an "industrial/non-slave state, a second new state was brought in as a "slave state below the line. In 1850 the whole thing fell apart because of California.

California Slaves

157

California was an important state for a number of reasons. Not only was San Francisco becoming one of the largest towns in the country, but more importantly, a new breed of slaves was erupting that would begin to weaken the control of the Industrialist States if nothing was done. These "slaves" were from China and they were unique. They worked harder than black slaves and they were NOT CALLED slaves. Certainly, they were beaten if they ran off, were segregated from Normal Americans, were required to work longer hours than normal people, were not allowed to own land, and were not allowed to stake a claim for gold or minerals, but they were sort-of paid [less than a third of a Normal person] so no one had to say they were slaves. Anyone with half a brain would have recognized that this new type of slave would soon be instituted and the "Slave substitute" in the slave States to increase production and to eliminate the slave stigma. If that happened, the mid-western agrarian States would not be able to be controlled by the Industrialist Statettes and larger States in congress as farmers would vote with farmers if the slave issue had been settled.

California Causes Trouble

You would think that California was a huge territory that was essentially split in half by the Mason Dixon line of demarcation and would certainly be introduced as 2 States. If it had been introduced as two States, one above the line being non-slave and a second one below being a slave state, everything would have stayed calm for quite a few more years. By a substantial number of shenanigans, California was to be introduced as a single state rather than 2 States with 1/2 being for each side. There is absolutely no reason why the state wasn't split except that the industrialists [STATETTES] were gaining too much power. No one could stop an outcome that would give them more power. The spiral was downhill for the Agrarian States from then on, starting with the Kansas Civil War of 1855.

The Kansas Civil War of 1855

Here is how the real 4th Civil War started. The Kansas and Nebraska Territories had both come up for statehood so a new law was introduced that let those territories vote on their slavery preference. By coincidence, this was called the Kansas-Nebraska Act of 1854. Kansas was essentially put up for bid and both sides wanted the new state votes. The "anti-slavery" States and the "pro-slavery" States sent large quantities of people to vote on their side. The first vote was almost unanimous. The State was to become a slave state, but the congress of the United States did not accept the entry. If you remember California had just been introduced as 1 state instead of 2. Unfortunately for the United States, the reason given for not accepting the vote was because Kansas was situated at a latitude above the Mason Dixon line and not allowed to be a slave state by the Missouri Compromise Act of 1818. California had just entered statehood in complete violation to this same law and now the extra votes of the violating State were used to eliminate another "Slave allowed" state. Below is how the States and territories were divided up after the Kansas-Nebraska Act.

Two years later a new vote was initiated with more of both sides voting. This second vote changed the state to an anti-slavery state. Like the 1st vote, the second vote should have also been thrown out. Some try to say that not all of the voters were Kansas citizens. I think they were right. Let's look at the voting information.

159

	# of Kansas settlers	# of votes for slavery	# of anti-slave votes	Constitution Characteristic
1855	2800	??	Very few	Slavery
1857	2905	6320	Very few	Slavery
1859	~4000	5530	10,421	No Slavery

Anti-Slavery was not Pro-slave

Before we go father and look at the killing that occurred, let me say that anti-slavery sentiment did not mean citizens that were trying to help black Americans---absolutely NOT!!!!!!

> *The antislavery side wasn't out to eliminate slavery and they certainly didn't want the Black Americans to have any rights. They simply didn't want large plantation owners to limit white human jobs.*

To showplace this general feeling, local laws were enacted in Kansas and throughout many areas of the anti-slave States. The laws were essentially all the same they would not allow black Americans into their territory or community at all. One of the Senators of that time might have expressed these views quite eloquently. You might remember him. The senator was named Abraham Lincoln.

Lincoln Against Black Americans

To begin to paint a picture of the Lincoln character we need to go back in time a little. Just a few years before he was in the Senate, Lincoln had an opportunity to represent either side of a free black man and his "former" master dispute. Lincoln rejected the black man's petition and argued that the former master had the right to take the man's wife and children away as they were not people. Luckily, Lincoln's arguments didn't hold up and he lost. The man's wife and children were returned to him, but that type of action was continued throughout Lincoln's career and somehow, they are ignored in our classrooms today and you have heard a different story, but the facts don't support Lincoln as a black American helper. Here is what Lincoln had to say while he was a senator. This is a portion of a speech given October 16, 1858. What we find is that he consciously advocated racial supremacy. This is just a portion of one of his "Antislavery helps poor white Americans Speeches".

"Whether slavery shall go into Nebraska, or other new Territories, is not a matter of exclusive concern to the people who may go there. The whole nation is interested that the best use shall be made of these Territories. **We want them for homes of free white people.** *This they cannot be, to any considerable extent, if slavery shall be planted within them.* **Slave States are places for poor white people to remove from**, *not to remove to."*

Notice that he only desired slavery reduction so that poor "normal white Americans" could live and get jobs. I'm not sure what he thought would happen to the black "less important" Americans if slavery was abolished and the poor whites took their jobs. We know from his speeches that he didn't care what happened so long as it didn't happen in Nebraska.

Lincoln Gets Specific

Let's read further as Lincoln goes on the Presidential campaign again in 1858. Here we can see that, not only did Lincoln hold these views, but also the citizens that voted for him had similar views or he would not have been elected. This is from one of the debates with Stephen Douglas. It's his "Black people are subhuman speech".

"I will say then that I am not, nor ever have been, in favor of bringing about in any way the social and political equality of the white and black races - that I am not, nor ever have been, in favor

161

of making voters or jurors of Negroes, nor of qualifying them to hold office, nor to intermarry with white people.

Clearly, he viewed the Black-slave Americans as a subspecies. Again, he reiterated his feelings about Black Americans and it isn't pretty. Not only did he not want blacks to vote, be a juror, or hold any type of office, but he continued further addressing his desire for the WHITE RACE to rule over the BLACK RACE.

*I will say in addition to this that there is a physical difference between the white and black races which I believe will forever forbid the two races living together on terms of **social and political equality**. And inasmuch as they cannot so live, while they do remain together **there must be the position of superior and inferior, and I as much as any other man am in favor of having the superior position assigned to the white race**."*

If that doesn't show that he was a huge racist, I don't know what else to say.

End of the 3rd Civil War

This war was over in 1860, and there would not be another Civil war for at least another year. The next one is a really bad one so it will have its own section. First, we need to address science.

19th Century Scientists

Before I get into the fourth Civil War and get people angry, I think I'll bash scientists for a while. Surely, we have been told the truth about our great inventors of the 19th century. After all; if they made the light bulb, telephone or radio, they revolutionized our way of life today. But credit may not be directed properly. Let's investigate.

1809 Who Invented the Light Bulb?

I need to get back to bad mouthing scientists again and you probably guessed that Edison wasn't the one who invented the light bulb. He was the first to use tungsten as the emitter. **Seventy years** before his patent, an Englishman named **Sir Humphrey Davy** invented the first light bulb. It used a Platinum emitter. I wonder what "normal history" in England says? Edison is probably the bit player in that country. The following shows the progression of light bulbs and the inventors are indicated below each.

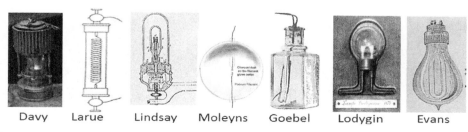

Davy   Larue   Lindsay   Moleyns   Goebel   Lodygin   Evans

The next group continues describing the progressive inventions of the common lightbulb. Please notice the Swan bulb using

163

carbonized paper. By partnership Edison took control of the Swan patents and the Latimer patents to make his own, copy. While we can't say he was a great inventor, he did know how to use patents.

Latimer   Swan   Maxim   Edison   Eidson/Swan company and their bulb

1890 Who Invented the Telephone?

It was actually a German physicist named **John Reis**. In fact, he did it in 1861, many years before Alexander Bell became famous with his copy. About the only change made by Bell was the use of a different voice diaphragm to increase the clarity. Our history books praise Bell. Probably German history books tell a different tale. The first phone is shown left and the Bell copy is shown right.

The Reis Telephone of 1861-The sound quality wasn't very good, but the device worked, just the same.

1892 Who Made the First Radio?

I guess you know it wasn't Marconi, because I purposefully picked things that have been changed by history books. In this case the inventor was **Nathan Stubblefield**. He demonstrated his device over a period of 10 years to many people, but unfortunately his patent '00600457" didn't keep others from stealing his invention. Many years later Marconi became our hero.

Nathan Stubblefield's Radio Transmitter-As the father of the Radio, he said. "I have perfected now the greatest invention the world has ever known. I've taken light from the air and the earth as I did with sound ... I want you to know about making a whole hillside blossom with light...". After that, he locked himself in his shack and starved himself to death. [See next left]

Sewing Machine Invention

Certainly, sewing would not threaten history and an accurate accounting could be written down, so who invented the sewing machine? If you said Elias Howe, you'd know who patented the idea of 1846, but many would say Isaac Singer, who was just a patent infringer from the 1850s. Both are wrong, of course. Ten years before the original patent, a man named Walter Hunt actually made one in New York, but he also wasn't the first either. It was actually invented by a Frenchman named

165

Barthelemy Thimmonier. In 1831, some of these sewing machines were purchased and used by the French Army, so it was like an inventor just coming up with a silly idea like many do today. There may be two reasons we don't remember him. He was French, but no one wants to admit when the French help us, and no one could spell his name so Howe and Singer became famous. [See previous right]

19th Century Scientific Protection

Besides all the glory stealing, nineteenth century scientists protected us by coming up with scientific facts to guide us. Of course, 20th century ones may be no better, but I think we are, at least, a little more enlightened today. He is a short list of their world controlling conclusions.

Physics-If a train goes faster than 21 MPH, the air will be sucked out and everyone will be suffocated.

Astronomy-No stones can fall from the sky, because there are no stones in the sky.

Aerodynamics-It was proven that things that are heavier than air cannot fly.

Medicine-The doctor's leeches were replaced with Laudanum [opium]. It started out as the cure for all coughs and ended up as the cure for everything.

Moleoscopy- The study of moles to determine the nature of a person was practiced as late as the 19th century. Some of its findings are listed below.

- o Mole on outside corner of eye-An honest person
- o Mole on bridge of nose-A lustful person
- o Mole on chin- A conscientious person
- o Mole on nipple- [either breast] A fickle person
- o Mole on left rib away from the nipple- A lazy person

166

o Mole Near the lip [See below] shows a benevolent nature.

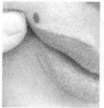  

Psysiognomy- When the mole thing didn't seem to track, people, including Hitler and the third Reich, used facial characteristics to determine nature of a person. Here are some of the findings. In the German case, a wrong head-shape could mean your death. [**It is all very scientific.**]

o Round head –An intuitive person

o Triangular head-An impractical, but quick thinking person

o Straight eyebrows- An alert and active person

o Arched eyebrows- A person with a great imagination

o **Large nose- An aggressive person**

o Narrow lips-An unemotional person

o Large earlobes-An independent person

o **No earlobes- A person who lacks sense of purpose**

o High forehead- An intellectual person

o Narrow forehead- A great analyst

o **Round eyes-A naïve person**

Complex machinery provided accurate indictors, but the science was just silly.

This science was no better than the Mole one, but it was used for many years even though some people without earlobes laughed at jokes. There is another thing 19th century science insisted. People could not be eaten by a whale and survive. Again, they were mistaken.

1891 Modern Jonah

What do James Bartley and a whale have in common? James was the only man, besides Jonah, to be swallowed by a whale and live. The date was 1891 and he was a whaler. He slipped at the wrong time and a sperm whale swallowed him whole. If that is not bizarre enough, he was in the whale for 15 hours before being removed. His skin had been bleached out and he had trouble with his vision, but he survived and the incident is well documented. This should be brought up whenever our children are told to read a fiction about a white whale named Moby Dick. As it turns out the Moby Dick book and the Bible provide more truth than is currently being attested to.

Hopefully this section has made to understand that you need to dig to find the truth. You can never simply accept what people tell you even if they are trusted educators or scientists. There is a slight possibility that 19th century scientists and historians did not know the whole truth and that is why there are so many vastly differing stories to be found about even 19th Century America. If we are looking for truth about our heritage during this time period, the whole question about slavery and a huge war that was supposedly fought over it must be readdressed. Let me start with Slavery in general.

Slavery Established Our Country

What I mean by the title of this section is that people sold themselves into slavery or were sent to the Americas as punishment from a war and the quantity of these individuals was enormous. Sometimes people called it "indentured servitude" but it was basically the same thing as slavery. In many areas, there were more white slaves than black ones. At least **seventy percent** of migrants to the Chesapeake Bay region, the Caribbean, and Virginia arrived as "white indentured servant/slaves". Most were unmarried men who were enslaved involuntarily or who had sold themselves to get to the new world and were enslaved for periods of up to 12 years and often longer. To extend the number of years, the servants were encouraged to borrow against their servitude time. You guessed it. Many never became free men.

Irish Slavery

The infamous Cromwell sent an estimated **70 thousand** Irish woman and children into slavery in the West Indies, but many, many more were just as unlucky and found themselves slaves one day without a Cromwell to blame. Like the Black slaves sent from Africa, many of these white slaves died during the passage, and during the term of indenture. If a master got tired of a particular "worker" he could sell the remaining period of indenture of any white slave, much like any other slave. That is not to say it wasn't worse for the black slaves, because it was. Not only did they have the slavery against them, they also had the "subhuman" remarks of those like Abraham Lincoln and a slew of others to contend with. In this section I was not trying to discount other forms of slavery, but I do think that we need to understand the big picture of slavery in America. For those against Cromwell slavery was real. The big picture for black slaves includes England and France as the major players.

Black Slave POWs

It seemed like Africans were trying to destroy Africa during this terrible age. Just as one group would win one war and take away slaves, another group would beat the winning group and they would become slaves themselves. This was the African form of genocide and it was substantially different that Hitler's. Instead of killing the losers, the winners made money with them and still accomplished the same genocide. There was no reason to have huge prisons or even huge execution areas. This slave thing made warring easy and efficient. The groups that made out the most from the Africans killing each other and driving each other into slavery were the English and the French.

British and French Slavers

The English and French black slave trade occurred between 1450 and 1900.They were good at it and made a great deal of money selling slaves. They stacked the unfortunate prisoners of the African Wars like sardines. The round objects in the ship diagram above are heads. On this particular ship there were an estimated 433 slaves. The slavers even made special fake money called "Popo Manila" to give to the Africans in payment for their captured enemy. It was a terrible time and a terrible outcome of the African tribal wars and Muslim enslavement.

If you are wondering just how many slave POWs were exported from Africa, during this 450-year period there were over 11 Million Africans that were transported around the world. Here's the part to remember with respect to American History. Only 4% of them were sold to the colonists and North America. The rest found their way to other, not so pleasant, areas. Below is a list of those totals.

Region	# of Slaves	%
West Indies	4,100,000	36.4
Brazil	4,000,000	35.4
Spanish Empire	2,500,000	22.1
USA	500,000	4.4
Europe	200,000	1.8

There is one thing to note from the table above.

Most black slaves in the United States did not come from Africa. They were true Americans.

Only 500 thousand African slaves were brought to the United States colonies over the entire 450 years of the African slave trade. All the rest were born in the United States. President Jefferson had outlawed the practice of receiving slaves from another country in 1808 so most of the depictions of slave-ships continually coming to North America carrying sardine packed slaves is not a complete picture.

The percentage of slaves to non-slaves was continuously decreasing. As shown below, the slave population was 18% of the total population in 1800 [not including indentured servants] and the percentage had dropped to only 13% by 1860.

For those thinking the North and South ideals were substantially different we should note that the drop was about the same in both north and south with about a 4% drop in percentage of slave population experienced in both the north and south. Certainly, there were more slaves in the Agrarian sections of the country, but the thing to look at here was that the numbers were going down.

Slave Use Growth	1800	1810	1840	1860
Slaves north [M]	.2	.2	.4	.4
Free north [M]	3	3.8	9.6	20.3
Slaves south [M]	.7	.9	2	3.2
Free south [M]	1.2	1.8	5	7
% slaves north	6%	6%	4%	2%
% slaves south	35%	33%	30%	31%

Generally, slaves were not being brought to the United States for sale, nor was the use of slaves the major reasoning behind the 4th Civil War. One of the major reasons for the 4th Civil War was the same thing that was responsible for what we call Manifest Destiny.

Manifest "Malarkey" Destiny

In the 1840s, everyone was counting on the United States to expand to California, but it was not destiny that drove the action, it was good old American greed. Don't let anyone tell you any different. Land speculators with strong government connections would purchase or take over large plots of land at the edges of a territory or "outside the United States". Then they would get a friend to get a friend to cause the United States boundaries to be expanded. Once the expansion was done, the land could be sold for HUGE profits to farmers. These weren't the huge slave owning plantation farmers, these were the, "I've barely got enough to live on" farmers.

Land Scheme Makes the Railroaders Wealthy-Those with the right friends became extremely wealthy because of this Manifest Destiny thing. The land selling scam was one of the major reasons that those "investing" in railroads became so very, very wealthy during this time. Somehow the classroom discussions seem to center around Manifest Destiny as this exclamation that people had and this idealistic goal of fate. It wasn't like that at all and they should quit teaching that way. My apologies for the outburst. Anyway, let's continue with trying to define what caused the 5th Civil War in America.

Causes of the 5th Civil War of 1861

The details of this particular time period in American history has become so skewed that I was forced to write a stand- alone book specifically addressing this war. This section will provide the highlights that are important as we examine human existence and specifically American existence through the 19ᵗʰ century. The Civil War was the most significant war to Americans with respect to loss of life, loss of freedom, loss of dignity, and loss of historical correctness. Some of the misconceptions deal with slavery so some will get angry and some misconceptions deal with illegal congressional voting so others will get angry, but we need to remember our past or we will never control our future. So go ahead and get angry, but read the information first. Like the others before it, this war was fought over the same problems, it just escalated beyond what the others had done.

The war was fought over three things; greed, corruption, tariffs, and representation. Somehow people always talk about slavery.

Greed Caused the War

I'm sure most have heard the term **"follow the money"**. It works in almost all situations and this one is no different. The farmers and the southern farm States did not gain in wealth so the other States or some shrewd manipulators who would gain from a war must be to blame. I know some don't believe it so let's look at the evidence. Below are personal property values of 8 States from the 1860 census and ten years later. Make no mistake a state cannot increase its actual worth by over 400 percent immediately after a war unless some shinnanigans was going on. Note that the States

173

were equivalent before the war, but the war brought unbelievable wealth to a very select few.

South	1860 [$B]	1870 [$B]	North	1860 [$B]	1870 [$B]
S.C.	0.4	0.18	Mass.	0.3	2.0*
N.C.	0.4	0.13	N.Y.	0.7	2.0*
Miss.	0.5	0.18	Ohio	0.3	1.8*
Ala.	0.55	0.16	Penn.	0.5	1.8*
Total	1.85	0.65	Total	1.8	7.6
Inc.		-65%	Inc.		422%

[* approximated because the census numbers were capped at $1 billion]

Tariffs Caused the War

This war was similar to the others with respect to cause, but it was the only "Civil War" that turned into a country crippling war. To know what happened, we need to go back in time about 40 years before the war. This "Tariff War" actually started back in 1820.

Tariff	What it meant to Agrarian States
Land Act of 1820	This lowered the worth of farmer's land. Decreasing the power of the farming community while increasing the power of the industrialist groups.
Tariff of 1828	This placed tariffs on raw material made in the south while not affecting finished goods produced by the Statettes.
Protection tariff of 1832	This increased rather than decreased the raw material tariffs.
Tariff Force Bill of 1833	This was enacted to force the Agrarian States to follow the unacceptable tariffs.
Morrill Tariff of March 1861	This raised the average raw material tariff rate from about 15 percent to 37.5 percent.
Lincoln Tariff of April 1861	Under a deal to get himself elected, Lincoln raised the tariffs again to an unbelievable 47 percent.

Just think about what you would do if your taxes went from 15% to 47% in a matter of months when you believed that the 15% level was so harsh that you had banded together with your fellow misery feelers in 1833 and were unsuccessful in reducing the torture below the 15% mark.

British Viewpoint

174

In England, the causes of the war were well known, but in America, the cause of slavery overshadowed the other issues. Here is what they said.

> *From "British Times" [1862]* *"The war between the North and South is a tariff war. The war is, further, not for any principle, does not touch the question of slavery and in fact turns on Northern lust for sovereignty--is a mere tariff war, a war between a protectionist system and a free trade system, and Britain naturally stands on the side of free trade."*

Corruption Caused the War

A very few, highly motivated and less than honorable individuals used their influence to increase their wealth and power. While they didn't necessarily try to make people kill each other. The killing was, apparently deemed a necessary evil to a common goal. That goal was control of the United States.

> *Oh, did I mention that Lincoln's 47 percent tariff produced the richest men ever in America?*

Some may recognize the short list of instigators that follows, but this is only the top of a well-defined group that used slavery, fear, and ignorance to increase their power. The short list below is by wealth only. Before the War they were wealthy and manipulating, but by the end of the war these men were fabulously wealthy and completely controlled the United States for all intent and purpose.

By the way, I am not picking on wealthy men so that the slavery issue will be softened. These guys were bad. On the one hand they thrust our country into the fastest moving Industrial Revolution of the world but it was at a terrible, and unthinkable price that almost destroyed our liberties. Later in life most of these individuals had something in common. They felt so bad about what they had done, that they became philanthropic. People forgot about how bad they were and only remembered how much of what they stole was given back to Americans.

The Man or Family	Richness rating
John D. Rockefeller	1st
Andrew Carnegie	2nd
Cornelius Vanderbilt	3rd
Andrew & Richard Mellon	5th [together]
A. T. Stewart	7th
Frederick Weyerhaeuser	8th
Jay Gould	9th

It should also be noted that these few are not the only culprits. Of the 38 richest men EVER in America 80% of them gained their wealth during the period between 1850 and 1870. During the first 10 years of this period the presidency was owned by Northeastern men who tried to enhance the wealth of that sector of our country. During the remaining 24 years, the presidency was owned by an almost unchallenged Republican Party that almost exclusively represented the Northeastern States and Statettes.

Here comes the part that people soften. Without a challenger, the country slipped away from a democratic country to a fascist State. Only by the remorse of the super wealthy at the end of this period was our country finally saved from destruction. A brief overview of each of the above "gentlemen" is given below. Remember that these are only the tip of the corrupt iceberg.

John D. Rockefeller [1st]

Good old Rockefeller started out in oil. To enhance his power, he made a secret deal with the Vanderbilt railroads. He would get "under the table rebates" for transporting his oil that no other oil company got until he almost wiped them all out. Rockefeller gave away huge sums of money later in his life as restitution, but the damage that he and his fellow instigating manipulators could never be made up. Do not admire this man.

Andrew Carnegie [2nd]

176

If you convince the government to build railroads over the entire land and completely control the steel market, you can ask any price for your goods. This is especially true if the government places extremely high tariffs on any incoming steel. I'm certainly not saying that Carnegie tried and was successful in swaying congress to go against the people and help him in this venture. All I'm saying is following the money brings us to him very quickly. Like Rockefeller, Carnegie felt so much remorse for what he had done, he gave away huge sums of money away later in his life as restitution. Do not admire this man.

Let's review

- Of the 38 richest people in America EVER, ¾ of them made their wealth between 1850 and 1880.

- Those 30 years were tenuous for most Americans. A huge depression seized our country, but the 30 men making up the richest of the rich couldn't be more thrilled at the control they had over the government.

- If we were to further breakdown the reasons for wealth, we find that many became wealthy in the exclusive club called the railroad. If they didn't make it directly, they made it by selling steel to the railroads, or wood for ties, or providing funding necessary to support the railroad ventures.

- The government overly supported railroadians. They gave them land, funding, grants, guarantees, prizes for laying rail, exclusive rights to determine who could transport goods on their railroads.

- There is a high probability that the government did not provide these things to aid the country. The only ones who were aided were the 30-man exclusive club of the mid-19th century.

Some might think that they must have had inappropriate influence on the government that almost destroyed our great nation.

> *The corrupt governmental manipulation provided their wealth. It was not the industrialist cunning of an entrepreneur, but the criminal actions of a fascist society controller.*

Sorry for the meanness again.

The Top Three Controllers

The three most notable people to take advantage and manipulate the laws during this time were Cornelius Vanderbilt, Andrew Carnegie, and John Rockefeller. As shown in the table above; with the right manipulations, these three "Gentlemen" became richer than any other American before or since their time.

> *John Rockefeller manipulated the oil market. Carnegie had steel for the railroads, and controlled the telegraphs. Vanderbilt controlled shipping and the Railroads.*

If there had been a word like Fascism during this time, these men would have defined it, worked it, and reaped the benefits of it. I'm going to briefly provide an overview of some of the people in the 30-man club, with particular attention on the three main instigators as corrupt leaders. We simply have to start with the worst of the worst whose name was Cornelius Vanderbilt.

Railroad Money

I've already discussed some of the "scandals" associated with Vanderbilt, shown below left, and his railroads, but more should be brought out so that we get a better picture of things that weren't considered scandalous. Four of the five transcontinental railroads were built with **free assistance** from the federal government through land grants. Receiving **millions** of acres of public lands from the post war Congress, the railroads were assured land on which to lay the tracks and land to sell, the proceeds of which helped the poor and innocent companies finance the construction of their railroads. The railroads, then divided the continent into five freight rate territories. The "Official Territory", which consisted of the non-agrarian States east of the Mississippi, enjoyed the lowest freight rates for manufactured goods and the "Southern Territory", which consisted of the Old Confederacy, including Kentucky that had declared neutrality, enjoyed the highest freight rates for manufactured goods. The railroads contended that manufactured goods originating in the South were very expensive to transport but that raw materials destined for northern factories were not as difficult to transport. Northern manufactures could ship goods from New York to Athens, Georgia cheaper than a manufacturer in Atlanta could ship the same goods to Athens. The U.S. Supreme Court held that the rate structure was in violation of the Sherman Antitrust Act but the Interstate Commerce Commission made a new ruling that price fixing was allowable as long as it was voluntary. Of course, neither had any affect until the 1880s, so Mr. Vanderbilt got free land, got free antitrust law violations, and added to the destitution of the southern States along with the benefits of actions deemed as

179

scandals. Certainly, Vanderbilt [next left] wasn't the only Railroad manipulator and we will look at a few more as we go along.

Jay Gould

In 1863, Jay Gould [Above middle] became manager of the Rensselaer & Saratoga railway and President Grant's Brother-in Law. From his earnings, he bought Rutland & Washington railway. He became a broker in railway stocks and joined with James Fisk to take control of the Erie railroad. From 1868-1870, Gould manipulated stock prices and sold $5 million in fraudulent stock. In August 1869, Gould began to buy gold in an attempt to corner the market, culminating in the panic of Black Friday, on September 24, 1869. The price of gold fell 30% in one day and many people were ruined—not Jay.

Edward Henry Harriman

Like most of the unbelievably rich "industrialists", and I use that word not as a complement, Harriman was born in 1848 and like the others he made his wealth because of and during the 5th Civil War. He was a high school drop out by age 14 and made his mark on Wall Street message boy. By the 1870's he was well under way and turned to the almost certain wealth machine called the Railroads. By 1881, his name was synonymous with "railroad." Don't, for a minute, think that he wasn't involved in the Vanderbilt railroad scandals I mentioned before. [above right]

James J. Hill

Like the others, Hill was born in 1838. He made his fortune in three areas. The first was a railroad line as there was always some good governmental support for the poor industrialists controlling the railroads. The second was fuel. Railroad fuels and land were his other "government supported" money makers. As for the fuels, he obtained a company with exclusive rights to sell coal to the railroads. Now that's a good company. He wasn't through there either. [Following left]

Our Government Helping the Poor

During the time when the railroad companies had convinced "America" to have a transcontinental railroad, Hill pushed his railroad workers so hard that the government gave him a small gift. Hill received two million acres of land in the Minnesota Land Grant for completing the rail line on time. Hill was able to sell this gift for $2.50 to $5 an acre making him one of the richest men in the United States.

Collis Potter Huntington

Mr. Huntington was born in 1821, about the same time as the other "lucky" industrialists. In the late 1850's, he and 3 other "businessmen" formed the Central Pacific Railroad Company to create the western link of America's transcontinental railway system. Four additional Rail systems were brought into control of this group with Huntington at the lead. The good old government gave him massive amounts of land making him one of the country's largest landholders. Those gifts and the other incredible grants given to the poor railroaders made him slightly wealthy. [Next middle]

Frederick Weyerhauser

Finally, let's examine Frederick Weyerhauser [Previous right]. He was getting rich by supplying timber from his sawmills and knew a good thing. He essentially bought or leased most of Wisconsin, Minnesota, Idaho, Washington and Oregon to supply wood for the railroads and everyone else. I have no idea how he came to control such a huge piece of our country, but he wasn't complaining.

Steel and Money

If you convince the government to build railroads over the entire land and completely control the steel market, you can ask any price for your goods. This is especially true if the government places extremely high tariffs on any incoming steel. I'm certainly not saying that Carnegie, shown below left, tried and was successful in swaying congress to go against the people and help him in this venture. All I'm saying is following the money brings us to him very quickly. Of course, his partner, Frick might have also influenced the congress as both became unbelievably wealthy during this delicate time. Oh, did I mention that the country plunged into an economic Depression while these guys were getting filthy rich!

Henry Clay Frick

Again, we find that another of the richest Americans ever was born in 1849. Frick, shown above middle, began buying coal mines and sold the output to Andrew Carnegie. Eventually, he controlled 80 per cent of the coal output of Pennsylvania. Frick was also in control of Carnegie's Steel Mills for a time and decided the workers were being paid too much. Only 16 men were killed in the uprising that ensued, but Frick did make the company more profitable. Even after being stabbed 2 times and shot 3 times, he still survived and continued in his mindless attempt at put wealth in the hands of his very few friends. Frick, like many of the other men we have been studying felt terribly guilty at what he had done to get his money, but died before the real donations began. Nearly all of his $22 Billion [2004 equivalent] estate was donated to charities at his death, but that does not mean he was a great man. He was evil and bad just like the others on this special list.

Oil Money

Good old Rockefeller, shown preceding right, just had to get in the act and made a secret deal with the Vanderbilt railroads. He would get "under the table rebates" for transporting his oil that no other oil company got until he almost wiped them all out. Because his shipping price was so much lower than everyone else's, he charged less and the others simply faded away. The supporters of the old Sherman antitrust Act again would have been appalled, but as I mentioned above, that didn't even come about until the 1880s and the crooked congress turned their heads so they would stay popular with the powerful people and, of course, get money for the exercise. While most of the data should be tied to John Rockefeller, William Rockefeller was most likely in on most of the shenanigans as was Henry Rogers and Oliver Payne. [Sort of an oily group].

Oliver Hazard Payne

During the Civil War years, he became the 3rd largest oil refiner and went on from there. He did this by joining the "industrialist club". He joined with John Rockefeller, and the tone was set. The 26th wealthiest man miraculously made his money quickly. He became known as one of the Standard Oil inner group. As the government tried to come away from the Fascist Regimes [sorry for the term again] of President Grant and his successors, there came into being a new tool called the antitrust laws. While this did split Standard Oil into smaller companies, the conglomerate became even larger. Payne became even richer after the split.

Banking and Retail

While Andrew Mellon, shown preceding middle, only had a $32 billion fortune, combining his fortune and his brother's wealth together brings them to number 5 in all-time money getters, so we should look at the mid to late 19th century banking industry. It would be hard for anyone to believe that the banking industry used inappropriate government manipulation to further its goals, but apparently, it did. Their father controlled the Bank of Pittsburgh and so the two brothers continued in his footsteps. During the "Industrial Revolution", attaching to the right groups was paramount. They had helped Frick in his coal mining ventures and were rewarded with continued ties to Frick and Carnegie's Steel Companies. This union insured their wealth. The whole railroad steel thing and the direct scandals and indirect "should-have-been-scandals" brought them wealth in the post war era. Because the money was borrowed by the Carnegie's and others in the group, repayment was <u>assured by the federal government</u> and the Mellons made billions.

John Pierpont Morgan

Here is a name we can remember. John Pierpont Morgan [preceding right] ran the wholesale banks during this time of what some call opportunity. He was the most responsible man for

185

bankrolling the Railroad billionaires. At one time, Morgan was said to have had more influence than the President but his power waned towards the end of his life in particular following investigations into his banking practices. Can you imagine that! He only had an estate worth about $25 Billion. Surely, he would not have gotten the money inappropriately and would not have been involved in any of the multitude of scandals of the day.

A.T. Stewart and Retail Store Money

The above greedy and despicable men weren't the only ones eager to take control during the desperate times in the last half of the 19th century. A man named A.T. Stewart began his rule of the department stores of America by supplying the Union soldiers with all types of goods to be shipped by **railroads**. [Can you begin to see a connection?] The hallway in his house is depicted with the previous images-right. Notice how the railroad industry seems to be the center of all the wealth of this time, even when we are trying to look at stores. Like so many of these men, this guilt-ridden man donated millions of dollars to the "normal" people before his death. Why he felt he should, is what people should be asking rather than praising his unusual philanthropy.

Marshall Field

Speaking of stores; what about the other large department store of the time? Marshall Field is the guy controlling the department store world. While the most reasonable explanation for his skyrocket to the "Wealthy Club" was some underhanded connection with the rest of the gang, no direct link has been made, but he would have had to have some close ties to the railroadians or he could not have gotten his goods to market efficiently. Remember almost all the other store owners of the times were going though one of the worst depressions of the United States.

Less Than Honorable

Without any effort, at all we find that more fabulously wealthy people became rich during this Civil War period and the Fascist years that followed than at any other time of our history before or since. I mean more wealth than will ever be seen in our country again. Thirty out of 38 came for this time. That doesn't mean that men are no longer entrepreneurial nor does it mean that the men during this time were more skilled. It also doesn't mean that this time was a period of affluence for America, because it was a disastrous time and America was crumbling while the protected few took advantage of the Republican strong arm.

ANYONE trying to tell you they made their money because of entrepreneurial spirit should never play games in Las Vegas.

I only briefly discussed some of the inappropriate, underhanded, country destroying, un-American actions that were provided to Mr. Vanderbilt and the others so that they could get rich, but the real shenanigans these men must have gone through to acquire this wealth may never be known because they were, in essence, the legislative decision makers for industry and the legislative decision makers for the entire country during this fragile time. Many call these "less than honorable men" great. The only reason I can see that people believe in their greatness is they are blinded by our histories not reporting history. I can't put great by these men. I have a hard time seeing past the unbelievable lust for power.

Slam Bam Something Happened! -Again, I must bring up an unusual fact. Later in life most of these men became extremely sorrowful and began to give away large amounts of their wealth, so the question may be, "Why did they feel they had to do such a thing?" The question should never be, "How could these men have been so great?" There is a reason why these men felt so

187

guilty all of a sudden. I simply don't know what it was. In the late 1880s Carnegie, Rockefeller, Stewart and many, many more of these guys started giving away the money that they had gotten. The exclusive club that had been taking from the Americans more than anyone in recent past suddenly had a change of heart. They supported the antitrust laws as well to ensure that no one would do what they had done in the past and no one seems to be wondering what happened. There is no record of the confrontations these men must have gone through. There is no record of these men being visited by some higher being. The only thing we know is that what they were doing was COMPLETELY out of character and if they had not done it the country was about to fall apart. It saved America.

Cynicism Noted-I know I sound like a cynic and the paragraphs above do not absolutely show their un-American connections of these men. What I really want everyone to know is that the United States, as we know it, was almost destroyed. It wasn't by the Civil War, but by what happened while the war was going on and immediately afterwards as the agrarian States lost all control and a very few Industrialists took over the nation for a time. The party in power was the Republican Party, but that does not mean that the Republican Party will destroy our country, it means that the Congressmen elected during that time as puppets of the Industrialists were destroying our nation.

If democracy is to survive, we must have at least two powerful parties fighting for goals different than the other. If we ever lose the evenness of power between the republican and democrat parties or whatever parties that are most influential at the time, we will, again, put our country in jeopardy.

With that, let me focus on how the War Started.

Statettes Caused the War

I addressed unfair tariffs and greed as major issues of all the Civil Wars, but the thing that allowed these things to blossom should be considered as the "real cause" of the 5th Civil War. The real problem was the same problem that caused the first 4 civil wars. That problem was the unequal representation of the statettes. The United States was becoming self-sufficient and the crops of the southern States were responsible for a major portion of that prosperity. Eventually, cotton and other industrial type crops were supporting major portions of the nation, but the "agrarian States" were split up into huge chunks of land when compared with the so called "industrial States". Rhode Island, Connecticut, New Hampshire, Vermont, New Jersey, Massachusetts, and Delaware combined together were smaller and had less influence on the nation's economy than Virginia and most of the other suffering agrarians States.

Equitable Representation was eliminated because of the tiny statettes. Something should have been done about it a long time ago.

Rather than combining these **tiny "statettes"** into one or two reasonably sized States and allowing for some semblance of equality in representation, the infinite wisdom of the industrial revolutionary controllers, who lived in the statettes, claimed that industrial States should have more representation "just because". Then they said something totally absurd. They said that the House of Representatives equalized the inequalities which were a totally untrue belief. While the House of Representatives being determined by population does HELP in the equalization of representation; the representation of the Agrarians in this country was poor because large chunks of land [meaning lower Senatorial

189

representation] were used to bring money to the nation and it was done with relatively few people [meaning lower Representation in the House.]

Without the "economic worth" of a state as a factor, New Hampshire and the others became overly wealthy with respect to representation and the Agrarians believed that they had to fight or their way of life would come to an end. When I say way of life I don't mean life with slaves. Jefferson had already outlawed the importation of slaves into the United States and the time of slaves was slowly coming to an end with or without the war. The Southern States knew equal representation of the Agrarian States was coming to an end, so they initiated a revolt to separate away from the "statettes" of the North.

Why the Statettes are not blamed is beyond me!!

By the way, please note that every year, the state sizes were forced to be larger. This was obviously done to enhance the power of the Eastern Coast community at the expense of the western States. Am I the only one that can see this injustice for what it is or am I all wet thinking that Texas is larger than Rhode Island?

All new States were required to be substantially larger than Rhode Island to insure power was held by the northeast.

One more thing! The statettes are still not combined and still have inappropriate representation, so we are still in trouble. While greed, limited representation and tariffs did cause the war, there is something that did not directly cause the United States' most bloody war. The thing that didn't cause it was slavery.

Slavery Didn't Cause the War

If you don't believe that the previously described gentlemen were the instigators of the war, at least understand that slavery was not

190

the reason. Almost everyone, including many of the 375 thousand slave owners in the South knew and even supported the dissolution of slavery. I know that there were a few bad apples that had found new fortunes in selling slaves, but I'm talking about the majority here not the insane. Speaking of crazies, the southern States contained 10 million people and of those people less than 6 percent owned the 3.5 million slaves.

Initially all the original States were founded with slavery being legal and 15 States had already changed their laws to halt the terrible practice. Almost every year another state was added to the non-slave ranks. There was never an incident that suggested that States would revert back to slave acceptance after the inevitable transition and more and more of the planters in the south were abandoning slavery as the only means to support their harvest. Many were finding that indentured workers and even migrant temporary harvesters could be worked harder and, many times, with lower costs, so the "south" would, most definitely, have been converted in a short time.

Slavery wasn't the major driver for the unrest in our country, but because the industrialist manipulators pushed this subject, for the sake of greed alone, it caused the small farmers to become confused concerning what side of the "industrialist versus agrarian" fight they should be on. Some agrarian States voted with the industrialists so that they would not be considered as slavers and the manipulators in the statettes laughed each time that they gained more control. The culmination was the secession of 10 ½ States from the Union, our 4th and most devastating Civil War, a tremendous political power boost for the miniature statettes in the northeast, and some of the richest Americans of all time.

This one would be a bad one and anti-slavery became the battle cry. State survival and representation power were always the only two issues. Slavery simply got caught up with the other two.

191

Possibly the most obvious reason the whole slave thing doesn't make sense is that about 1/3 of the Union States were slave owning States. In fact, there were almost as many States with slave owners on the Union side [8 ½] as there were on the Rebel side [10 ½].

Slaves in the North

It is true that the agrarians used and abused slaves and it is true that certain legislation had been passed which put pressure on the slave States, but what is not typically noted is that the agrarian States began to be a major influence on the country as a whole and that influence did not provide the agrarian States reasonable representation. Another element that seems to slip away is that some of the "agrarian slave States" sided with the Union during the war. The small group of only 10 ½ States went up against the other 20 ½ States that made up the United States and 8 ½ of the Union States had slave owners.

About 15 percent of the 3.8 million slaves in the United States were owned and traded by the "Union side" during the war.

These northern slaves were mostly located in the following union States: Nebraska, Kentucky, New York, New Jersey, Washington DC, Delaware, Maryland, West Virginia, and Missouri. The table below shows the quantity of "northern" slaves that were allowed to stay slaves.

Northern State	# of Slaves	Northern State	# of Slaves
Kentucky	210,000	Nebraska	10,000
W. Virginia	150,000	DC	3,000
Maryland	90,000	Delaware	2,500
Missouri	87,000	New York	500
		New Jersey	250

If that table doesn't show that slavery wasn't the main issue, I made a second one. The table below shows the various proportions of slave States to States without slaves. There are just about as many slave owning States on the Union side as there was on the "Rebel" side.

Union States without slaves	With slaves	Rebellion States
Maine & N. H.	W. ½ Virginia	Florida
Connecticut & R.I.	Maryland	S.C. & N.C.
Vt. & Massachusetts	Wash. DC	Georgia
Minnesota	Kentucky	E. ½ Virginia
Pennsylvania	New York	Alabama
Michigan	Delaware	Mississippi
California	Missouri	Tennessee
Kansas	New Jersey	Louisiana
Iowa	Nebraska	Texas
		Arkansas

Kentucky, W. Virginia & Washington D.C. Stand Out

Besides there being the occasional slave in the North; if we look at Kentucky, a full 23% of the families owned slaves according to the 1860 census and West Virginia had an even higher percentage at around 30%. So there can be little doubt that slavery was an accepted part of life well outside the Rebel States. Oh Yeah! Washington D.C. had an estimated slave population of 50% to top the list.

Tennessee Stands Out

Did I mention that one of the "Rebel States" outlawed slavery? With Tennessee becoming an anti-slave state, that was 10 percent of the Rebel States were against slavery and still the war was called the slave war.

Free Black Americans Stand Out

Here is still another piece of information. According to the 1860 census, there were over 130 thousand free black Americans living in the various "rebel" States before the war started [about 3.5% of the black population]. While that number is appallingly low, it was getting larger every year as slavery was becoming a thing of the past.

The War

The 4th Civil War began and the killing started. By the time the war was done, about one million men had become its casualties. The southern States had almost none of the railroad systems for transport, only about 1/3 the population, about ½ the number of troops, and very little industry. ---Guess who lost. While the war lasted for about 1600 days, it took about twice as long as it should have to destroy the place as it did because of disease.

Disease

Disease was responsible for twice as many deaths as bullets as shown in the tables below. The first shows Deaths from direct kills and from amputation infection. The second shows various diseases.

Bullets

	# Hit N/S [x1000]	Deaths North	Deaths South	Treatment	Totals x1000
Direct Kill Bullets	185	110	75	none	185
Limb Shot	60	10	10	Amputation	20
Total killed	205	120	85		205
Wounded	480				480

Bugs

	Infected N/S [x1000]	Death North	Death South	Treatment	Totals x1000
Diarrhea & Dysentery	3800	80	50	Mercury & Chalk	130
Typhoid Fever [Salmonella]	1000	50	40	Quinine & Whiskey	90
Pneumonia	2500	50	40	Hot Food	90
Rheumatism	2000	20	18	Electric Shock	38
Malaria	1500	10	6	Quinine & Whiskey	16
Measles, TB, & Smallpox	700	20	12	Vaccination & Whiskey	32
other	700	20	14	Rest	34
Totals		280	180		430

194

The 1877 Deal

I'm not really going to get into the war because it is covered in another book, but the beginning of the end needs to be addressed. If the war wasn't bad enough, the recovery from the war was just as bad or worse and it lasted 3 times as long. During much of the recovery time, the entire country was faced with an almost unbearable Depression. Except for 30 of the 38 richest men ever in America who "flourished during this time, the mood of the country was downtrodden and solemn. U.S. Grant had almost single-handedly turned the country into the very essence of a Fascist Society as he was played like a puppet for the fabulously wealthy industrialists. Without the Agrarian counterpoint, the Industrialist control of the country was unchallenged and the country was devastated.

A Miracle Happened

Like a miracle, many of these "super wealthy 30" had a change of heart and tried to make restitution to the country. Most started giving their money away while some even supported a democratic presidential candidate named Tilden. This all happened around 1875 and Tilden would have won the election. An unbelievable deal was made and President Hayes became President even though he lost the election to Tilden by 300 thousand votes. Hayes promised to repatriate the South if Tilden stepped away. Hayes honored his word and ordered the withdrawal of the United States troops from the South. Very quickly, democrats regained the State governments and some semblance of order finally was found within the misery of the South and the rest of the country. Why these things happened is beyond me and should be addressed in more detail, however, we must go on and simply say it happened for now as we try to understand the big picture of the American society. I know that I seemed to be picking on the rich in this section, but it was not my intent. It was forced out as I tried to investigate the facts. The 30 rich guys I previously mentioned were the driving force behind the Industrial Revolution. Many have been told the Industrial Revolution was a good thing and it certainly was good for the 30 individuals listed below.

Rank	Name of Industrialist	Birth/ death dates	Source of wealth	Estate $Billion
1	John D. Rockefeller	1839-1937	oil	190
25	Henry H Rogers	1840-1909	oil	25
26	Oliver Hazard Payne	1839-1917	oil	25
38	William Rockefeller	1841-1922	oil	17
2	Andrew Carnegie	1835-1919	steel for railroads	101
3	Cornelius Vanderbilt	1794-1877	railroads	96
9	Frederick Weyerhaeuser	1834-1914	lumber for railroads	43
10	Jay Gould	1836-1892	railroads	42
20	John Blair	1802-1899	railroads	29
24	Edward Henry Harriman	1848-1909	railroads	25
27	Henry Clay Frick	1849-1919	steel for railroads	22
28	Collis Potter Huntington	1821-1900	railroads	22
33	Mark Hopkins	1813-1878	railroads	20
35	Leland Stanford	1824-1893	railroads	18
37	James J. Hill	1838-1916	railroads	17
5	Andrew W. Mellon	1855-1937	Banking for steel	32
5	Richard B. Mellon	1858-1933	Banking for steel	32
18	Moses Taylor	1806-1882	banking	29
19	Russel Sage	1816-1906	finance	29
23	John Pierpont Morgan	1837-1913	Finance for railroads	25
36	Hetty Green [woman]	1834-1916	investing	17
11	Marshall Field	1834-1906	Retail stores	41
8	A.T. Stewart	1803-1876	Retail stores	47
16	James G. Fair	1831-1894	Mining gold	30
32	James C. Flood	1826-1889	Mining silver	20
17	William Weightman	1813-1904	chemicals	29
21	Cyrus Curtis	1850-1933	publishing	26
29	Peter A. Widener	1834-1915	streetcars	21
31	Philip Danforth Armour	1832-1901	Meat packing	20
34	Edward Clark	1811-1882	sewing machines	18

The table is of the richest men in America before 2008. I already discussed 7 of them previously. This list is grouped by industry rather than ranking and the estate worth is in today's dollars. You have to have at least $17 billion to even get on this list and there are only 8 members who didn't get their money from the Civil

War. Three made their billions in the ugly land deals of the late 18th century and 5 have become fabulously wealthy in the 20th century. All others made their wealth from the 5th Civil War. OK! James Fair and James Flood would have been wealthy no matter what happened because they found gold and silver [a lot of it].

When I say that the Industrial Revolution was a bad thing, I don't mean that making industry was bad, I mean that using any means to suppress people's rights is wrong, especially when the endeavor helps such a very few individuals. You can tell when something is abnormal because it only occurs in an isolated area, time, or to a small population.

Industrial Revolution

If you look at history there are always anomalies. For instance, it is strange that the Industrial Revolution really only occurred in a significant way in the UK and in U.S.A. While I don't want to belabor this event, I do want to reduce its glamour. The Industrial Revolutions occurred because of Imperialism and the Civil War.

England Used Imperialism

In England, the Industrial Revolution was fueled by imperialism. In the second half of the 19th century they obtained the following countries-Malaya, Burma, Thailand, Egypt, British Somaliland, almost the entire southern portion of Africa, Sudan, Uganda, Kenya, Rhodesia, Bechuanaland Protectorate, Basutoland, Nigeria, Australia, New Zealand, Hawaii, Western Samoa, Fiji, and Cyprus. So much new industry was necessary to hold on to and run such a diverse set of people around the world that, by necessity, industrialization was lauded by the people even though much hardship was thrust upon the populace to enter into this mass expansion of technology.

U.S.A Used the Civil War

The Civil War and the after-war corrupt government brought the industrial revolution to America. All of the power in our country was shifted to the industrial States and statettes. Because the Industrial Statettes had so much power, laws, acts, and amendments were passed which made industrialization flourish and the agrarian culture die. Unbelievable scandals erupted to extend the profit motive to new heights. If you remember, I said we need to "Follow the Money" to get to the meat of the problem. The 7 special individuals discussed previously and most of the others in the elite group indicated previously manipulated the government into a single industrial machine. The only thing that mattered was making more wealth by the establishment of very controlled industries at the expense of American freedoms. We made it through our Industrial Revolution and survived, but it could just as easily have ended without much pleasantness.

We aren't a great nation because of the Industrial Revolution, but in spite of it.

Besides the strange remorse felt by the industrialists in the 1870s the other reason we survived is internal imperialism. That is, our country began spreading out west to counteract the effects of the industrial revolutionaries. With the expansion came new freedoms and its own set of problems.

Spreading West

I know I stated the Manifest Destiny was a thing controlled by greed, but it also helped save our country. Many of the people that began migrating to the industrialist centers of our country found out it was not wonderful for the workers so, out of desperation, our inhabitants began pushing towards the west. By spreading west we collected many new natural resources that kept us alive during this delicate time.

With all of the weapons designed for the Civil War and the Vanderbilt railroads, this group of Americans quickly took over the area that was once owned by the American Indians. For centuries, the Indian tribes had been used to annihilating one tribe and then another tribe annihilating the victors, but this time the annihilations of Indian tribes were considered bad because the killings were done by "outsiders".

Many people today feel that the white people had no business killing red people. Only red people were supposed to kill red people, or at least, that is what red people told each other. Our schools even promoted the unfair notion that white people killed

200

defenseless red people. I'm not talking about how Abraham Lincoln killed 38 "redskins" in the largest mass execution ever in 1861, in fact that incident should be remembered and is not. I'm talking about how the educators and congressional leaders seem to insist that we should be ashamed for the actions of the slaughtering, westward pushing, settlers who were pitted against the defenseless Indians

Shame Denotes Payment

We are generally taught that if we were really ashamed, we should give the remaining Indians special privileges like building casinos, getting federal money every year [forever], not paying taxes, and allowing them to kill eagles. To emphasize this notion, nasty white people that do the things that are restricted for Indians are put in prison. After all, the terrible white people killed Indians over a hundred years ago and their skin color isn't right.

If any of the people who are <u>against</u> giving black skinned Americans money [Reparations] because their ancestors were slaves and believe that the American Indians are somehow different and <u>should</u> get special reparations, I feel sorry for them.

Indian Countries

If I haven't gotten everyone angry already, I'm going to get some more people angry, but I just can't help it because a more unbiased [OK! Somewhat unbiased] history must be presented and Americans should be treated as equally as possible. Black and Red Americans should not get special treatment.

Here is my dilemma with our Indian relations; we sort of gave the Indians small "countries/ reservations" as **reward for loosing** because we didn't know what else to do with them. For whatever reason, these countries didn't appear to be self-sufficient, so we took care of the reservations and the Indians on them. The big problem is--- **we have never stopped**.

201

I think the second method is best. If they were given land for our past shame, make the land U.S. land again just like land owned by the other "Americans" who actually pay for the privilege of living on a piece of U.S. land; make them pay the same type of taxes; and make them follow the same laws of the land. If that is not desirable, completely separate those sections and make them pay for the privilege of using our roads, telephone systems, and all the other things that make American life better than most life styles around the world. Don't get me wrong. I know that the American Indians as a whole are some of the poorest "semi-Americans", but the "semi" part needs to be removed.

Indians Not letting Americans build and/or use roads

By the way, this thing about the Indian reservation officials holding Americans hostage in New Mexico, recently, by indicating that roads would not be allowed to cross their reservation/country unless Americans paid dearly for that privilege shows our stupidity. That sort of thing brings out how very dumb it is to allow these countries inside our country to survive.

Italy isn't still paying Etruscans for taking their land. England doesn't pay the Vikings. The Cherokee Indians don't even pay the ancient Adena Indians that were almost annihilated to allow for Cherokee expansion. Before that, the Adena didn't pay the Aztlan Indians whenever their country was overrun. No nation practices such absurdity. It is simply wrong and historians seem to ignore the injustice simply because the American Indians are

202

portrayed as a victim still after hundreds of years. Let's use the Indian logic on the Southern States after the Civil War loss.

Today we spend about $1.5 Billion dollars a year on "foreign aid to the Indian countries" under what is called the Bureau of Indian Affairs.

Even with that, the Indians are aided from other non-Indian assistance and welfare programs and about 50% of the 2 million Indians in the United States live inside the Indian Reservation/countries where each family member including children are essentially given about 60 acres of land without charge. To top it off, we gave them back the right to vote outside their country without requiring them to conform to the laws of the United States.

The Agrarian Reservation

What if the outcome of the Civil War was to provide safe haven for the "Rebels". We could have made the land below the Mason Dixon line and east of the Mississippi a "Rebel Reservation". The rebels would have lost, but now the land would be theirs for free and as payment for the war and taking away their livelihood, we could have taken care of them with grants and other support similar to that which we provide to the American Indians. Then we could have allowed this Southern Reservation to have gambling casinos and things like that. We wouldn't let them have representation, but they didn't get representation after the war anyway. We also would not charge them taxes and they could make up their own set of laws. Don't you think that would have been great and make a lot of sense?

Post War Indian Countries

From the chart below, notice that all our cities and residential areas for 98.5% of the people only add up to 4.3% of the land that makes up the United States or 98 million acres. This is about _**0.3 acres per person**_ and business. The vast majority of the land is

203

"secret land" where no living, working, residential-ing, or urbanizing is done. That is another story not covered in this book. The remaining 1.5% of the "quasi American red-people" get 56 million acres or *12.5 acres per person* given to them rent free, tax free, and almost law free. Yes, I'm talking mean about the American Indians.

	Acres [M]	% of Total
Not Indian, business, or residential land	2127	93.2 %
Non-Indian Residential and Business Land. 98% of the people live work and die on this part of the United States.	98	4.3%
Indian Reservations [1.5% of the people]	56	2.5%

The strange thing is that it isn't just one piece of land. It is hundreds of pieces. The American Government sends money to the residents. That might be OK if we got something for our money or if we were doing it for our citizens, but these people are above some of the laws that people who are not getting free land and yearly payments must abide by. Certainly, the "freedom" everyone knows is that these countries can have gambling inside their countries regardless of what the laws of the country are. Everyone has also heard about how these above the law quasi-citizens can also kill American Eagles without the normal repercussions. There are 304 different types of "reservation living groups" that are treated in this special way and given countries inside the United States Boundaries. Twenty-one of the blocks of land are larger than the State of Rhode Island. Several are larger than 3 or 4 of the Northeastern Statettes so sometimes we are talking about huge pieces of land. Other plots of land are small where a special group decided that they liked a different area than the large Indian countries. Remember we are talking about 588 pieces of land scattered all over the place. [That's **588 internal countries** that live outside our law, but with HUGE foreign aid].

204

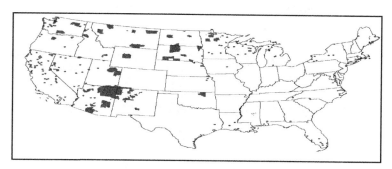

The picture above shows the **422 "country-ettes"** that are scattered around the main portion of our country and no one seems to care. Many of the land areas are worth substantial amounts of money, especially the **83 country-ettes inside the State of California**. These guys don't pay Federal, State income taxes or even sales taxes if they have business dealing inside their countries, but we pay them money every year to keep them enslaved. This is wrong.

As we move away from sense, let's look briefly at our Presidents. Some of their actions didn't make much sense. Most of this upcoming data is not earth shattering, but it may give us a better picture of this section of history.

U.S. Presidents

Here's a pop quiz concerning the most notable group in our US History called Presidents. Many of these important events are not taught in schools, so I'm giving the answers with the questions. Ok; some are not very important events, but they are interesting just the same.

Illegal Presidents?

Besides any of the Presidents that took office before the Constitution was adopted, how many Presidents were not born in the United States of America? If you guessed 8 you would be correct, even though people try to indicate that a President must be born in the United States of America to become President these "evil" ones slipped by the odd requirement and became President anyway. [That was a joke!]

- George Washington
- John Adams
- Thomas Jefferson
- James Madison
- James Monroe
- John Quincy Adams
- Andrew Jackson
- William Henry Harrison

Besides this short list several were born in areas that became part of the United States after they were born so they also could be considered bad.

Patriotic Presidents

Of all the wars, there were more Presidents in the one we call the Civil War. I suppose one could say it was a great honor, but many were drafted. How many Presidents served in the Civil War? [Seven is the answer.]

- Andrew Johnson - Civil War

206

- Ulysses Grant - Mexican War and the Civil War
- Rutherford Hayes - Civil War
- James Garfield - Civil War
- Chester Arthur - Civil War
- Benjamin Harrison - Civil War
- William McKinley - Civil War

I know there were 7 Presidents in World War II also, but most did not see action. Here is that list just to keep the record straight.
- Dwight Eisenhower - WWII "General"
- John Kennedy - WWII
- Lyndon Johnson - WWII
- Richard Nixon - WWII
- Gerald Ford - WWII
- George Bush - WWII

Unreligious Presidents

Which 2 Presidents refused to become a member of any church? I give you a hint. One blamed the Civil War on God. His name was Abraham Lincoln.
- Abraham Lincoln
- Andrew Johnson

Cow President

Which president had cows brought to the White House so that they could graze and provide milk for the First Family?

- Andrew Johnson; who else. He was the first president to be lynched, first to be elected after being a slave, first to be almost impeached, first president to become a senator after his presidency.

Accidental President

Which president accidentally became president and survived two assassination attempts in which both assassins were women. A hint is that he was the only president to never be elected and the only president to have a position as a "male model" before

207

landing the bigger job. I'll even tell you his real name, Leslie King. Both he and his wife had been models prior to their new fame and both had changed their names.

- **Gerald Ford** took the Vice President spot when Spiro Agnew resigned and then he accidentally became president when Nixon left office. I have no idea why women tried to shoot him.

African American Presidents

Name the 6 African American Presidents. I'll even give you a hint. These guys were not full-blooded African, but were mixed blood Caucasian and African. Here is the list.

- Thomas Jefferson
- Andrew Jackson
- Abraham Lincoln
- Warren Harding
- Dwight Eisenhower
- Barack Obama/ Barry Soetoro

Makes you wonder why there was such a hubbub about Barrack Obama running in 2008 doesn't it? He also is a mixed bred guy just like these earlier African American Presidents.

The 12th President [sort-of]

Which president served the shortest time? Here's a hint. He actually only served one day in 1848.

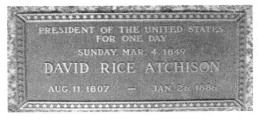

President Atchison [1848]

He served only one day. He was between James Polk and Zachary Taylor. The senate elected him because Zachary did want to take office on a Sunday, so there was a one-day delay between the two, more well-known presidents. It was a glorious day for President Atchison and very few scandals occurred during his presidency. David Atchison did have one scandal to contend with during his presidential reign. He, evidently, drank a little too much during the inaugural celebrations and reportedly slept his entire presidency.

Not the Shortest Reign as President

While only being President for 24 hours is short, his reign was by no means the shortest. Three times, the Vice Presidents have had to assume the power of the Presidency.

President G.H.W. Bush's first Assignment-Ronald Reagan had to undergo surgery on July 13*th*, 1985 for cancerous polyps near his colon. He wrote a letter to both the Speaker of the House and the President pro tempore, announcing his incapacity. Therefore, George H.W. Bush acted as President from 11:28 AM to 7:22 PM, when Reagan sent another letter, announcing he was once again capable of serving as president.

President Dick Cheney-The same situation occurred when George W. Bush underwent colonoscopy in 2002. Vice-President Dick Cheney acted as president for several hours. [June 29, 2002- 2 hour and 15 minutes]

President Dick Cheney's Second Term- In 2007 G.W Bush became ill again and Vice President Cheney became our president for a few hours again. [July 20, 2007 -2 hours and 4 minutes]

Family Presidency

What 19 presidents were related to FDR? If we aren't being taught that the presidency has being given to a very small representative sample of the American people, this one factor

209

should at least be addressed to show serious problems with our election system.

Teddy Roosevelt, of course, but also Washington, John and John Quincy Adams, James Madison, Martin Van Buren, the two Harrisons, Zachary Taylor, Grant, Taft, Cleveland, Nixon, Hoover, G & GW Bush, Pierce, Lincoln, and Ford.

- James Madison: half first cousin twice removed of George Washington
- John Quincy Adams: son of John Adams
- Zachary Taylor: second cousin of James Madison
- Grover Cleveland: sixth cousin once removed of Ulysses Grant
- Benjamin Harrison: grandson of William Henry Harrison
- Theodore Roosevelt: third cousin twice removed of Martin Van Buren
- Franklin Roosevelt: fourth cousin once removed of Ulysses Grant, fourth cousin three times removed of Zachary Taylor, fifth cousin of Theodore Roosevelt
- Richard Nixon: seventh cousin twice removed of William Taft, eighth cousin once removed of Herbert Hoover
- George Bush: fifth cousin four times removed of Franklin Pierce, seventh cousin three times removed of Theodore Roosevelt, seventh cousin four times removed of Abraham Lincoln, eleventh cousin once removed of Gerald Ford
- George W. Bush: son of George Bush

Sounds more like a kingship succession than a freely elected presidency doesn't it?

Besides President Atchison, there have been 43 presidents to GW Bush and about ½ of them are from the family of Roosevelt in some way.

A Real Rough Rider President

This has nothing to do with limited access to the presidency, but while we are talking about Teddy Roosevelt, what did he do "first" when he was shot in the chest?

- He finished his speech before he would let anyone give him aid. At another time, he also rode his horse 100 miles when the army personnel complained that the exercise requirements were too harsh. He was just plain tough.

First Woman President

Some may know this one. Edith Wilson, the wife of Woodrow Wilson, served as acting President for a full 1½ years. When her husband suffered a stroke, and because the Constitution had not yet been amended to appoint the Vice-President in his place, Mrs. Wilson handled the Presidential affairs, filling vacancies and administering foreign policy. Some called it the " Petticoat Government." but no matter what you call it Edith Wilson was our first female Presidential leader and should be remembered as such.

Scandal President

OK There are topo many, but the one who sold out and almost destroyed America in the 1860s was Grant so let's look at what he did that is covered up in textbooks.

U.S. Grant the Scandal Man

We should call Ulysses S. Grant the Scandal Man. During his presidency, leading Republican congressmen and officials, including those directly associated with the President, were involved in the Vanderbilt railroad scandals and many, many others, so is there any wonder that "Scandal man" was elected for two terms? Grant's Treasury secretary was collecting taxes illegally. His Secretary of War was taking graft for awarding contracts and his private secretary was skimming liquor taxes. Grant's Vice President, Henry Wilson, had a hand in a scheme to overcharge government rail-building projects. Fraud was widespread in the Departments of Interior, Indian Service and Treasury. His Attorney General and Secretary of the Interior were implicated in the Credit Mobilier railroad scandal, the most publicized crisis of the day, and that wasn't all. Here are just a few of the ones we should remember as "Scandal Man" worked his magic to insure a select group of Industrial Revolutionaries gained wealth beyond imagination.

Salary Grab Act Scandal

The whole Republican Party was implicated in the "salary grab" act of 1873, which retroactively increased the pay of congressmen and the executive. **Yes, that's right; President "Scandal Man" got more "inappropriate" money too.**

Star-Route Scandal

The "Star-Route" frauds involved <u>giving</u> lucrative mail transportation routes to particular Republican supporters.

Railroad "Credit Mobilier" Scandal

Credit Mobilier was a dummy construction company formed by the directors of the Union Pacific Railroad so that they could pay themselves inflated prices for the work that was done. **Because the "Republican" Congress paid the bills through generous subsidies worth millions of dollars, the directors made a fortune, especially one man named Cornelius Vanderbilt**. The more the line cost, the more money they made. Stock of the railroad was secretly transferred at a nominal price to various members of Congress and politicians shared in the profits after Congressman Oakes Ames sold stock in Credit Mobilier at discounted prices to his fellow members. One that we should remember who was on the take in this crime was Schuyler Colfax, the 1st Vice President of the United States under Grant.

Scandalous Railroad Subsidies

Every time I say the phrase "Federally Funded Railroad Subsidy" it makes me want to throw up. It was one of the richest money-making industries in America, at this time, but millions of subsidy dollars kept on being introduced and disseminated. While some of the inappropriate subsidies were finally noticed and removed, many of the subsidies never even exploded into the scandal arena, but Vanderbilt and his buddies kept getting richer.

Tweed Ring Scandal

This was essentially the exposure of the gigantic robberies in New York. The hoodlums were protected by their political connections. The robberies insured that no "inappropriate person" could get into the ranks of the super-rich. They channeled the wealth to a select group of individuals I call the Industrial Revolutionaries. Are you starting to believe that these "great", rich guys were not as great as the public believes them to have been?

Gold Market Scandal

I brought this up previously, but let me review this one. In 1869; Jay Gould, another one of those Industrial Revolutionaries; and

James Fisk, the scandal president's brother-in-law, attempted to corner the gold market. In furtherance of their scheme they persuaded President Grant to keep federal gold reserves out of circulation. Eventually, they wound up controlling enough of the available supply of gold in New York City to bid up the price to record levels. This made stocks soar and the Industrialists had enough money to buy any law or Act that they wanted. The way the story goes, once President Grant realized he'd been had, the federal government resumed the sale of gold, and the stock market crashed hard sending America into a Depression from 1873 until 1878.

Railroad Loan Scandal

During this time, high-flying bankers, like the Mellons, inappropriately made huge risky loans to railroad operators. This contributed to the worst economic collapse of the nineteenth century, commonly called the Panic of 1873. During the Panic, ten thousand businesses were forced to close. While you are thinking about the destitution of the "normal Americans" at this time, let me introduce you to the fact that during this same period, the apparent wealth of citizens of 4 States increased in their net worth by 400% average. [**Somebody must have been getting extremely wealthy as the rest of America was suffering. Don't you think? Let's look at that chart again.**]

North	1860 [$B]	1870 [$B]
Mass.	0.3	2.0*
N.Y.	0.7	2.0*
Ohio	0.3	1.8*
Penn.	0.5	1.8*
Total	1.8	7.6
Inc.		422%

Whiskey Ring Scandal

By 1875 it was found that a group of distillers and public officials conspired to defraud the federal government of liquor taxes. The ringleaders included "Scandal Grant's" chief secretary, who along with hundreds of others, were indicted. Many were convicted. Grant's secretary; however, was acquitted because he had some pretty influential friends. Soon after the Civil War these taxes were raised very high, in some cases to **eight times the price of the liquor**. Large distillers, chiefly in St. Louis, Milwaukee, and Chicago, bribed government officials in order to retain the tax proceeds. The Whiskey Ring was a public scandal, but it was considered impregnable because of its strong political connections. In the end, over $3 million in taxes was recovered, and of 238 persons indicted 110 were convicted. Many people, today believe that the Whiskey Ring was part of a **plot to finance the Republican Party** to further skew the government towards the extremely rich industrial revolutionaries.

Indian Ring Scandal

As the name suggests, this scandal involved Indians. Government provided food meant for the Indians in the Dakotas. Somehow, this food was converted into rotten food. At the same time, influential Grant supporters, at a very nice profit, sold the good food.

Indian Agency Scandal

Along with the above problem, in 1875, Scandal Man's Secretary of War, Congress impeached Belknap, on a charge of fraud and speculation in the disposal of Indian post traderships. The Senate acquitted him, but one man campaigned against him and gained Grant's hatred as he testified against Belknap and implicated Grant's own brother. We should remember his name as he will come up later. He was George Armstrong Custer.

I'm sorry, I keep writing about republicans as a bad group, because they are not bad, but during this time period, they seemed to be as close to terrible as I can believe for elected officials supposedly interested in the welfare of Americans.

Little Big Horn Scandal

From the above two scandals you can be sure that the Indians were getting restless and desperate so Custer was called in. He wasn't called in because Grant believed in his capabilities. It is now believed that Custer may not have died by chance at the Big Horn massacre. Due to the unbelievable nature of "Custer's Last Stand" it is becoming very evident that Grant's administration was directly involved in his death on June 25, 1876. Here are a few of the anomalies that don't seem to have answers unless we implicate the President.

- The fact that NO military aid was given to Custer and his 197 soldiers initiates disbelief and the crazy story that Custer tried to ride in alone to get the glory, doesn't make sense either. He was a glory hound, but he was also a great tactician and would have known the folly in that maneuver.

- The only reason Custer would have engaged such a large enemy was that he fully believed the two armies with him would join the fight. They simply allowed the massacre to continue.

- Given the fact that all military personnel that simply watched or heard Custer and his men getting slaughtered were not disciplined in any way, strengthens an uneasy notion. [I know the Reno's men had a hard time of it as well, but the whole thing sounds fishy.]

- The fact that the government supplied rapid-fire Winchester rifle to the Indians involved just before the incident feeds our doubts, especially when we find that Custer's men were supplied with single shot rifles.

- The fact that Custer was evidently ordered to leave behind his gattling guns seems very peculiar.

- The fact that all telegraph communications between Washington and the two armies to the north and south of Custer have been destroyed doesn't make sense.

- Other items that go all the way to the executive office make it pretty clear that President Grant was involved in a plot.

Essence of the Plot-This plot was to force Indians into war so that the Government could take the Black Hills, full of gold, from the Indians. The unfortunate sacrificial lamb was the unknowing "Grant antagonist" we know as General Custer. You could almost call Grant a murderer in this one. Even if he was not directly tied to the murder let's give Grant the memory he deserves.

Scandal Man was Truly NOT a Great American President. He should have been impeached and sent to prison. The people who try to excuse this man's actions saying he was just stupid don't understand that he took an oath to protect the Americans, he participated in many of the scandals, and he almost destroyed America.

Other Parts of the World

I know the preceding portion of the book seems to only be about American humans and I hope you recognize the reason for the time spent on the time period between 1830 and 1880 in the United States. Our American histories have been mangled when reporting this 50-year period and information had to be introduced. Besides, I know more about United States History. If we are going to look at other areas, we first need to step back for a little and catch up the rest of the world. I'm not going to go into a lot of detail, but it may be important to hit a few topics to keep some level of perspective. Our first stop is China.

China and Mongolia

You won't believe this but during the 12th through the 19th centuries, things were happening in other parts of the world besides the U.S.A. I'm not going to touch on much outside the United States in this book, but some is definitely necessary. Many were killing each other in massive, sometimes genocidic Wars, but the effect to the Westerners from most of this fighting was limited. For instance, the Chinese became powerful in their own rite mostly by staying by themselves. Here are a few of the high points including their engineering, their Tatars, and their Trojan Horse.

Chinese Engineering

The Chinese didn't simply put up a 6000 meter long wall and go to sleep, but because of their isolationism, their history doesn't play a substantial role in the western world. Some of the inventions certainly were important and eventually copied by the "outsiders". Here are a few that show these were amazing people.

- 1400BC- The Chinese invented the **decimal system** and 2400 years later, the Europeans decided it was a good thing.
- 400BC- The Chinese devised a **horse collar** that wouldn't choke the horse. 1200 years later, the Europeans came up with the same idea.
- 400BC- The Chinese started **Casting Iron** and 1600 years later the Europeans discovered Iron Casting.
- 400BC- The Chinese came up with the **kite** and were using them in war well before the Europeans who waited another 2000 years to discover this unique item.

- 200BC- The Chinese discovered that **blood circulated** throughout the body. The Europeans discovered it 1800 years later.
- 100BC-The Chinese came up with the **wheelbarrow** which became a European invention 1300 years later.
- 100BC- Chinese discovered a great way to make **paper**. In Europe it took another 1300 years to perfect.
- 100AD-The Chinese invented the **seismograph** and the western world came up with one 1800 years later.
- 400AD-The **helicopter** or at least the rotary wing was discovered and made into a child's toy by the Chinese, but it would take another 1400 years before westerners would take the toy and turn it into a helicopter.
- 600AD- The Chinese invented **Matches** and used them, but the Europeans could get one struck for another thousand years.
- 900AD- The Chinese invented **paper money**, but the rest of the world wouldn't begin to use this invention for another 700 years.
- 1100AD-The Chinese invented **rockets**, but they were not used in Europe until 1380.

Following is a more complete list of Chinese discoveries put together by well-known researcher, Herbie Brennan.

Gunpowder	Guns	Helicopter propellers
Hermetic sealing	Horse Harness	Hexagonal snow structure
Hot-air balloon	Immunization	Phosphorescent paint
Kites	Land Mines	Paddle wheeled boats
Land Sailing	Magic lanterns	Magnetic resonance
Magnetic induction	Manned Flight	Mercator map projection
Masts and sailing	Matches	Modern seed drills
Mechanical clocks	Mortars	Multistage Rockets
Paper	Paper money	Spontaneous combustion
Parachutes	Playing cards	Steel manufacture
Porcelain	Printing	Rotary winnowing fans
Relief maps	Repeating guns	Spinning wheels
Rudders	Sea Mines	Sliding calipers
Stirrups	Umbrellas	Suspension bridges
Underwater salvage	Use of Natural Gas	Use of Thyroid Hormone
Value of pi	Wheelbarrows	Watertight ship compartments

Other inventions were surely accomplished by this wonderful group of people, but they were so far away from everyone else, that nobody noticed until the Tartars came along.

Chinese Tatars

Of course, the Chinese didn't completely stay by themselves. Instead we find Tatars. As a brief chronology of the continuous warring before the 18th century, I am going to concentrate on these Tatars, just because I think it's an interesting name for a group of people. TATERS, TATERS, TATERs.... The Tatars were part of the Mongols that first went west to conquer and then took over much of China and Russia. I like the word Tatar, so I'm going to use it in place of Mongols. The whole group gets mixed up together, but here are some of the highlights that are not generally brought out.

- Mongols [I mean Taters] and the Ottoman go back and forth

- By the 13th century it is the Tatars turned and destroyed Baghdad as they started their quest for world domination. As part of this drive, one Tartar named Timur even occupied Moscow. The Mongols were in control of just about the entire Middle East and China.

- By the 16th century, The Tatars split up into several pieces and Ivan the Terrible took over most of the pieces. The Ottoman Empire was now in control of the Middle East and parts of China.

- About that same time the Crimean Tatars came together and sacked Moscow again, but soon the Tatars were defeated. Later a fun guy named Stalin even had some fun killing many of them. Tatars still occupy parts of the Ukraine, but they are nothing compared to the mighty Tatars of the past.

OK, that was a really brief overview, but I really only wanted you to remember that there were people in other regions than the Mediterranean Sea area. One of the things this great group should be remembered for is the Chinese, or Tatar version of the Trojan Horse.

Chinese Trojan Horse

This section possibly should be called the Trojan Virgin instead of horse. It starts with the beginning of an Ottoman Invasion. When the Ottomans started trying to take over the Tatar land they ran into some problems. In the "History of Ghewond", we find that an Arab general sent an insulting letter to the king demanding taxes and 30,000 virgins. The money was for him and the virgins were for his men. OK! Some of the virgins were for him also. The history indicates that the ruler got the 30 thousand correct, but instead of virgins, he concealed 30,000 warriors in covered sedans. At the appropriate moment the soldiers sprang out and massacred the Arabs--No kiss and no loving. The old Trojan Horse trick still worked as well for them as it had done for the Greeks and Egyptians and the virgins were safe for another day.

Europe

15th Century Europe

That is enough Oriental discussion, but I should address a couple of issues in regards to the 15th century Europeans. In this section we will look at just a few historically modified elements including those involving kilts, Newton, and DaVinci. That doesn't mean there weren't many more, enhancements, but I think the point that history should not be simply accepted can be made with these few.

The Kilt & the English-It might be hard to believe, but Scotsman didn't wear kilts even though we always see them in those outfits. They simply couldn't afford such a thing. Instead they wore very long shirts and a belt. The kilt wasn't even invented until 1727 and here's the kicker. An "Englishman" which was another reason for Scotsmen to shun them invented kilts. Even fashion history was changed to make life more picturesque. Now, get rid of the kilt image and picture Scotsmen dressed in long shirts if you want a more historically correct vision.

Da Vinci & Lisa-I don't want to leave anyone out in this discussion of how wrong our histories are so let me briefly talk about a painter. Leonardo Da Vinci spent 4 years on the painting we sometimes call the Mona Lisa. The question might be, "How many Mona Lisa's does one paint in 4 years?" If you said 60 you're pretty insightful as that is today's estimate. Here are a few of the better-known Mona Lisa's. The first is part of the Lord Spencer collection. The second one can be found in the London's museum. The third is in the Louvre. All are presumed to be authentic. The first one shows her naked. I don't know if Leonardo got in trouble with her husband for this one, but most have clothes. With 60 paintings to choose from, I imagine quite a few people own the original Mona Lisa.

Newton & Fermented Metal-[Back to picking on inventors.] In order to make Newton an idol of wisdom, our history of him stops with the drop of an apple and no one typically challenges how he and a German named Gottfried Leibniz came up with calculus at exactly the same time. We should look closely at our idols. Here is one of Newton's fantastic theories. He stated, "If base metal was allowed to ferment, it would turn into gold." Sometimes I think his brain was fermented just a little. By the way the apple drop story evidently was a true one by all accounts. Also let it be known that I have been trying to ferment some metal to get gold and I have had no good results.

18th and 19th Century Europe

In order to catch Europe up to the 19th century, we need to look at several more icons. Jonathan Swift, Napoleon, and the Victorian Age all highlight Europe of this time period, so let's look a all three. Not as normal history items, but as misrepresented elements of history.

Swift Moon's-Not too long after Newton discussed fermenting metals, a satirical writer came along. We all know about his book, but some may not have seen his far-reaching insight. In 1726, the writer Jonathan Swift somehow knew about Martian moons when no one else had any idea. In his "Gulliver's Travels", speaking of the fictional Laputans that were beings who flew around the skies in flying cities, he indicated that—

"-- they had discovered two lesser stars or satellites, which revolve about Mars; whereof the innermost is distant from the

223

center of the primary planet exactly three of the diameters, and the outermost five; the former revolves in the space of ten hours, and the latter in twenty-one and a half; so that the squares of their periodical times are very near the same proportion with the cubes of their distance from the center of Mars; which evidently shows them to be governed by the same law of gravitation, that influences the other heavenly bodies."

One hundred and fifty years later, the Martian moons were "rediscovered" by Asaph Hall. Even the revolution distances of both of the moons were correct. I don't know how Swift knew about these moons, but he was not guessing. Possibly he had some early manuscript about astronomy from before the Babel Wars. The thing I do know is that this portion of Swift's writing is not even in the "normal" book, that only deals with the giants and little people. Possibly it has been removed to keep people from asking about how he knew.

1799-1814 Napoleon-While Swift knew about Mars, Napoleon knew about Louisianna and found out about Russia. Let's get rid of some of the misconceptions. According to our standard version of history, this "short" man decided to take over the world and needed to get some money, so he stupidly sold "Louisiana" to President Jefferson, which increased the size of the United States by 33%. With the money he made Napoleon was able to attack England and the rest of Europe. With 600 thousand men he also went to Moscow. The Russians liked him so much that they burned down their capitol city and Napoleon almost lost all of his men because there was no food or shelter in the bitter cold. Later the stupid Germans did the same thing. They focused on taking over Russia. They attacked and died the same way that Napoleon's men died. You won't believe this but our concept of Napoleon has been skewed. Here are some problems with our memory of Napoleon. According to an autopsy report, Napoleon was five foot two based on the French "Pieds de roi" form of measurement. That would make him about Five foot six inches tall by today's standards which was better than average size for a Frenchman at that time, and the winter of 1812 was one of the mildest ever in Russia. The main reason his army was destroyed was that the supply-line distance was simply too long to be supported. His men died of disease, nor cold. In fact, many died in the hot Russian summer of that year.

Napoleon & Jefferson-Probably the most important thing that is misrepresented in our histories when reading about Napoleon is that Jefferson had **illegally** bought "Louisiana" with money "illegally" taken from money loaned to the United States from England, so Napoleon attacked Europe with English money given to him under the table by the Americans.

By the way, Jefferson's illegal dealing did give us areas that became 13 different States and I don't mean those tiny statettes.

Napoleon the Counterfeiter-Napoleon didn't get enough money for his conquests from the English, so he made more. He counterfeited currency to pay his troops so they were paid very well. By the time they found out, Napoleon already had other problems.

1800 Napoleon's Lazy-Susan-Here we get into his revolving discovery. Napoleon wasn't all bad as some may think and he was an inventor. One of his inventions was to make a sort of lazy-Susan for getting rid of unwanted children. This is one of the darker parts of history that no one likes, but we need to remember just the same. The church had outlawed killing children if the fetus was "completely" out of the womb, because thousands of babies were killed as they were being delivered. People enjoyed making the babies, but couldn't afford or didn't want the results. That, of course was an unending chain as people continued to make unwanted babies. Before Napoleon's invention they simply left the children in front of churches when they missed the "birth elimination opportunity". Many of the thousands of children abandoned this way, simply died because no one knew to look for the unfortunate children. The baby depositing people could not take the children inside the church or they might have been recognized. They could not take them into a hospital because they might have been arrested for their dastardly deed. ___Napoleon to the rescue!!___ He initiated the "**lazy-Susan, children elimination tray**" in front of the hospitals. With his invention, unwanted children were simply left on a portion of the tray that was outside the hospital and the tray was turned until the child went inside the hospital. The parents remained anonymous and the child survived. Thousands and thousands of children ended up this way in France, Spain, Italy and other parts of Europe. At one point it was estimated that 1/3 of all children were abandoned and Napoleon's invention was a huge success.

1840-1900 Victorian Age-Not only were people insensitive to children, but, in general, snobs abounded during this time. People wanted to be like Queen Victoria, who controlled her country well, but had absolutely no social life. To top it off, she was very "plain". People tried to become pale and plain just like her. Women drank arsenic to give themselves that pale, pasty look, which certainly worked as internal bleeding removed substantial portions of their blood. Queen Victoria, however, was no Victorian and really liked the old "booze". Not only did she like getting drunk often, but also, she had two husbands even though most histories remember only one and usually think of her as a spinster. Certainly, many other things happened in this era around the world, but most are somewhat reasonably reported and I don't need to repeat them here. One thing that was not actively reported, however, was stories of flying objects. No one wanted them to be real, but they didn't go away. Luckily, some people drew pictures of them. As we back up in history a little again, we can catch the essence of what people believed about flying objects as seen throughout the ages.

Flying Until the Middle Ages

In Book 3 we talked extensively about flying and, according to the Sumerian texts, the Nephilim stayed in some sort of flying city during the flood in order to protect themselves. Now the flood was gone. Also, the memory and vast use of flying machines had been lost to many. Even in this memory thing had taken over, the evidence suggests that some of the flying machines were still being seen. I'm not just talking about the sight described by Ezekiel, as many have read in the Bible, but the flying machines were seen around the world.

I'm guessing that "Normal" people did not have access to the flying machines after the flood. The use of these machines helped elevate the Nephilim to "god status" by the masses that were populating the world. Briefly, we discussed that drawings were made on the ground that only could be seen by the "gods' in these flying ships. These drawings are everywhere on the earth, but no place in more abundance than on the Nazca Plains in Peru. Let's see what these drawings show.

Drawings to the Sky

On the 37-mile-long, Nazca Plains, there are many representations of animals and long straight lines scattered over the desert. The lines were painstakingly placed for no apparent reason, unless they could be appreciated from the sky in flying ships. Modern people didn't even know they were there until about 1950 because they don't look like anything on the ground. Some of the lines go straight for miles. Even with mountains in the path, the lines are perfectly straight. How the lines were drawn is one question, but **why** is the more interesting thing to ask. Only someone from the sky could appreciate or use the lines. Here is a small sampling of the drawings in Nasca. There are many more which have been removed for easy viewing of the animals. The dotted line in the middle is where a road goes through the middle of the drawing. Recently, researchers have said that the people were able to do the work because they made primitive balloons, but that mean that other places with the same phenomenon would have had to know how to make these same "Balloons" as well. The "pictures" are found everywhere and balloon making people could not have been the makers.

Nasca is not the Only Place-In the UK, pictures of animals could only be seen from the sky and in Guatemala some kind of object that looks like a candelabra again is positioned so that it could not be seen. In the extreme north of Chile, you can see the image of a gigantic man 330 feet high. All across the United States are mounds that turned out to be pictures of animals that could only be seen from the sky. Everyone, evidently, knew about flying, whether they themselves flew or just made drawings for the gods that were flying in ships can only be guessed. Below are the famous candelabra and a horse that can be seen in the UK.

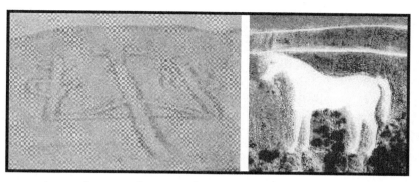

At some time, the people must have again been allowed to ride on and use some of the flying ships and from that type of vantage point, the ancient people were able to draw very incredible maps and confirm ancient stories about the round face of the earth. We looked at some of the maps in one of the previous chapters, but right now let's examine what the people saw in the sky. Our first stop is the Biblical history.

What I want to impress on you is that flying ships were common before and after the Tower of Babel incident.

Bible Flying

Our surviving Biblical texts are full of details about this mode of travel. One extremely detailed account in the Bible talks about 4 flying ships [wheels] seen at the same time. In that instance [Ezekiel 10], the "ships" were accompanied by 4 "fiery thrones". Many people have heard of this episode, but there are many more. Let's look at both the thrones and the wheels mentioned in ancient Hebrew texts in some detail.

Thrones and Fiery Chariots

The flying fiery chariots were all similar in that they were fiery, fast, and fearsome. The early Jewish people called these chariots, Merkaba, but while a name was given to them, they were forbidden to speak of them, so you have to wonder why the objects had a name. The early Jewish people might not have say the word merkaba, but they did draw them and write about them.

If you're interested in these flying ships, at least read one of the ancient Biblical books named Enoch. Notice that, in the book of Enoch, it clearly indicates that the ships went into space and that a huge ship was in orbit around the earth. Weird isn't it? We're trying to do that now.

2 Kings 2:11- And it came to pass, as they still went on, and talked, that, behold, there appeared a chariot of fire, and horses of fire, and parted them both asunder;

Enoch 74:15- I saw likewise the chariots of heaven, running in the world above to the gates in which the stars turn, which never set. One of these is greater than all which goes around the world. ***[This ship going around the world sounds similar to what we do today without space ships, doesn't it?]***

"The Divine Throne- Chariot"

For more detail, we need to look at the Book called "The Divine Throne-Chariot". The most detailed reference of a flying ship in ancient times comes from this particular book that was found among the Dead Sea Scrolls. Here is an excerpt from the ancient book. From this account, there can be little doubt that people witnessed flying ships after the flood. Here are just a few examples.

*Bless the image of the Throne-Chariot above the firmament, and - praise the majesty of the **fiery firmament beneath** the seat of his glory. **[Flames came out the bottom of the throne-chariot just like a rocket.]***

*And **between** the turning wheels, angels of holiness come and go, **[Angels ride inside the turning wheel.]***

*as it were a fiery vision -about them flow seeming **rivulets of fire**, like gleaming bronze, a radiance of many gorgeous colors, of marvelous pigments magnificently mingled.**[The flames shoot out in brilliant colors.]***

*Ascending they rise marvelously; settling, **they stay still. [It could hover and/or ascend in the air. This hovering thing is very interesting. Today we have found that high voltage charged devices float in the air just as this reference indicates. In book 8 we will look as some of these new discoveries.]***

The above describes is only one of the types of flying machines depicted by the ancients. Ezekiel and others apparently saw two main types of flying ships one that looked like a throne or chariot and another that looked like a wheel. It was a weird wheel that had eyes.

Wheels with Many-Eyes

You would think that most of the flying ships stayed in the Middle East. There are huge quantities of documents discussing them from India and everywhere in the Middle East, but to say the flying machines were concentrated in that one area would be a wrong statement. In the Americas, the flying chariot was also very common. We know this because they were used in ceremony by the kings of the day. We will look at the Americas in a minute, but right now we should look at the **second** most common flying device seen by the post Babel humans. The one depicted below is probably the one most seen today. The Adamics called it a Wheel in a wheel.

Like the description above, Ezekiel's description is exceptional. He said it was like a wheel inside a wheel with eyes all around. This sounds similar to many of the flying ships seen today. From Ezekiel's descriptions it seems that the eyes were many portholes. Unlike the chariot ship that was accompanied by a flame out its back, this one rose straight up into the air like a whirlwind.

*2 Kings 2:12- Elijah went up by a **whirlwind** into heaven. And Elisha saw it, and he cried, My father, my father, the chariot of Israel, and the horsemen thereof. And he saw him no more: and he took hold of his own. [**That was no ordinary whirlwind that Elijah rode in it was a flying ship.**]*

*Ezekiel 1:15-21- one wheel upon the Earth—was as- a wheel in the middle of a wheel. —their rings were high; and their rings were full of eyes round about them--- the living creature was in the wheels. [**These eyes could either be images of portal windows, or it could be a representation of a corona from a high voltage electric field.**]*

*Ezekiel 10:9-17- The appearance of the wheels was as the color of a beryl, they had one likeness, as if **a wheel had been in the midst of a wheel.** When they went, they went upon their four sides; they turned not as they went and the wheels, were full of eyes round about, it was cried unto them in my hearing, O wheel. They were lifted up: for the spirit of the living creature was in them.*

*Book of Abraham 8: 11-12- "I saw a chariot which had **wheels of fire and every wheel was full of eyes** all around and on the* *wheels was a throne and this was covered with fire that flowed all around.* [**This one seems to be a hybrid. The covered with fire image could very well be a corona image from an electric field.**]

Angels in Flying Ships

Although angels and possibly even Nephilim could apparently float, when it came to long distances, the written testimony indicates that they used the flying ships. The ancients provided us with a wide assortment of writings, drawings, and carvings that depicted these flying ships as described in detail in book three. Let's look at references to angels [gods] that used these flying ships to go places. These examples of angels seen in flying ships were witnessed after the flood and are from the Bible as well as Egyptian hieroglyphic Artifacts.

Ezekiel 10:20-22- They were the "cherubim". Everyone had four faces apiece, and every one four wings; and the likeness of the hands of a man was under their and the likeness of their faces was the same faces which I saw by the river of Chebar, their appearances and themselves: they went every one straight forward. [**These Cherubim were inside the throne seen by Ezekiel.**]

*Ezekiel 1:4-14- out of the midst of fire- **from the whirlwind- came four living creatures with four wings**, straight feet and they sparkled. Wings were joined one to another; -they turned not- they went every one straight- wings were stretched upward; two wings of every one was joined one to another, and two covered their bodies-their appearance was like burning coals of fire- **it went up and down—out of the fire went forth lightning**. They were as fast as lightning. [**The lightning image could have been exactly a lightning bolt or plasma string caused by extremely high electric fields used in the propulsion as discussed previously.**]*

233

Egyptian Hieroglyphics- *Osiris and Isis [gods] descended from the sky in a sun-ship, bringing wheat, and the arts of civilization to the world.*

American Flying Ships

On the other side of the world the same flying ships were also seen. In the Americas Flying ships resembled things we might see today. One type looked like a jet, one looked like a chariot, and a third looked like a rocket. They wrote about them drew them and even made models.

Written Evidence

In Peru, Alaska, U.S.A., and Brazil, ships from the sky were written about. The descriptions include features like a circular or boat-like frame, being made of metal, and having burning rays, or being bright. Here are some of the descriptions.

Peru Tradition-In their writings, the goddess Orejona landed in a great ship from the sky.

Chippewa Tradition-They told of the Gin-Gwin [Flying Boats] in their historical tales.

Navaho, Pintes, and Hopi-They all told of the Golden Strangers from the sky that came in flying canoes which were armed with Burning Rays. [**Laser weapons or lightning weapons?**]

Brazil, Manacitas Tribe-One of their cherished legends talks about the Macunbeiros, which were flying wizards that flew inside **circular,** luminous, machines. [**The indication of the craft being luminous may indicate an electric field corona.**]

Eskimo tradition-Their tradition states that they were brought to the north by gods with metal wings.

Drawn Flying Evidence

If you don't believe the written evidence, will you believe drawings from South America? Here are some convincing items.

235

The first device is the flying chariot of the King of Sipan. I know that a stupid cat is at the base of the chair, but the flames out the back are clearly shown in the drawing of this device. Clearly there are no poles for carrying, no horses for pulling, and no wheels; just flames out the rear.

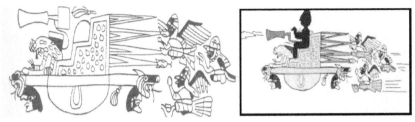

Three little roadster versions of this type of flying chariot were also depicted above. These also had no wheels and either flames or tail feathers out the rear. The drawing shows that flight was not only known about, it was probably commonplace. [**I put in some enhancements in the second figure to bring out the features of the chair.**]

Central American Confirmation

The Aztez and Olmec both showed what may have been rocket type flying ships as shown Next.

Codex Nattal-In the Nattal, one of the pictorial images clearly shows what is believed to be a rocket ship with thruster engines and flames. [Next left]

Olmec Rocket-The Olmecs carved this representation of a rocket-like object with the body of one of their gods at its base. This could have been a headdress if the person at the base was very, very strong, but I doubt it. [Middle above]

Another Olmec rocket-This representation is thought to be a missile piercing a mountain or some type of pointed object tunneling through a mountain, but to me it looks like a rocket that has been pierced.   [Above right]

Physical Evidence

A couple of the Columbian golden jets manufactured about 2 thousand years ago are shown below. They appear to be more like the jets of today which shows that the Americans had a wide assortment of air transportation possibilities.

If the Americans had all of these contraptions in the not too distant past, where are they today? Certainly, the metals would have disintegrated, but what happened to the knowledge about building them and are the ships we see today the newer versions of those used in the past? I think the answer might very well be yes.

Saucers Throughout History

Some people may discredit the extremely ancient writers because they saw angels at the same time that they saw flying ships and both are difficult to believe. Others discredit current sightings as part of a mass hysteria or desire to be in the limelight, but the same things have been witnessed throughout time. Here are a few of the more well-known recorded sightings by people. Most didn't necessarily see angels nor did they have anything to gain. These are not the Biblical references but are references from around the world. We start in China.

2200BC, Chinese used them- Emperor Shun reportedly not only made a flying ship, but also a parachute of sorts, 4200 years ago.

2000BC, Chinese built some- Emperor Tang wrote about a flying chariot that was built and flown. The craft was destroyed to keep the secrets away from outsiders.

1500BC, The Ethiopians saw them- According to the "Kabra Negast" [Ethiopian holy book] King Solomon would visit by flying on his "Heavenly Car".

1500 BC, Pharaohs saw them: As recorded, The Pharaoh Thutmose III saw silent, foul-smelling circles of fire and flying discs in the sky.

399 BC, Romans saw them- Julius Obsequens wrote in "Prodigia" about a number of Roman sightings, "-- a round object, like a globe, a round or circular shield, took its path in the sky from west to east.", another section reads," -- there came a terrific noise in the sky, and a globe of fire appeared burning in

238

the north. In the territory of Spoletum, a globe of fire, of golden color, fell to the earth gyrating. It then seemed to increase in size, rose from the earth and ascended into the sky, where it obscured the sun with its brilliance. It revolved toward the eastern quadrant of the sky."

329 BC, Macedoneans saw them- *Alexander the Great told of 2 great silver shields, spitting fire around the rims that dived repeatedly at his army as they were attempting crossing the Jaxartes River.*

300BC, Chinese saw them- *Chu Yuan wrote of a flight taken in a jade chariot at a high altitude over the Gobi Desert. He described how the ship was not affected by wind and how an aerial survey was performed, 2300 years ago.*

200BC, Chinese saw some more- *The historian, Ko-Hung, wrote about a flying craft with rotating blades to set the machine in motion [helicopter?]-2200 years ago.*

85 BC, more Romans saw them- *Pliny wrote about a sighting in, "Natural History: Book II", "--a burning shield scattering sparks ran across the sky."*

170BC to 100 AD, still more Romans saw them- *Conrad Wolfhart wrote about UFOs being seen a number of times during the Roman Empire in "Lycothenes", "At Lanupium, a remarkable spectacle of a fleet of ships was seen in the air. --wondrous flames were seen in the skies --Everywhere the air burned, -- a ship was seen in the air moving fast. At sunset, a burning shield passed over the sky at Rome. It came sparkling from the west and passed over to the east."*

May 21, 70 AD, Jewish Historians saw them- *Josephus wrote about a UFO in "Jewish War Book 111", "On the 21st of May a demonic phantom of incredible size...for before sunset there appeared in the air chariots and armed troops coursing through the clouds and surrounding the cities."*

239

320AD, the Chinese saw them again- *During the Han Dynasty Chang Heng made a "wooden bird" which flew for over a mile. Here is what Ko Hung had to say in 320AD. "Some have made flying cars with wood, using leather straps fashioned revolving blades to set the machine in motion."*

776 AD, the English saw them- *From English writer, W. R. Drake, we read, "-- they beheld the likeness of two large shields, reddish in color in motion above the church, and when the pagans who were outside saw this sign, they were at once thrown into confusion and terrified with fear and began to flee from the castle."*

810 AD, Chalemagne saw them- *The following was written down as part of an historical reference, "—he [Charlemagne] saw a large sphere descend like lightning from the sky. It traveled from east to west and was so bright it made the monarch's horse rear up so that Charlemagne fell and injured himself severely. [**First recorded UFO injury**]*

September 24 1235, Astronomers realize the truth- *General Yoritsume saw something strange in the sky,--lights in the sky were seen swinging, circling, and looping. Astronomers told him, "The whole thing is completely natural, General, it is only the wind making the stars sway".*

January 1, 1254, monks saw them- *A monk named Matthew of Paris, wrote, "--suddenly appeared in the sky a kind of large ship, elegantly shaped, and well-equipped of marvelous color. –finally, it began to disappear."*

November 4, 1332, more English saw them- *Robert of Reading wrote, "In the first hours of the night, there was seen in the skies over Uxbridge England, a pillar of fire the size of a small boat, pallid, and livid in color. It rose from the south, crossed the sky with a slow and grave motion, and went north. Out of the front of the pillar, a fervent red flame burst forth with great beams of light. Its speed increased and it flew through the air."*

October 11 1492, 10:00 PM Columbus saw them- *According to "The Life and Voyages of Christopher Columbus." Columbus and Pedro Gutierrez, while on the deck of the Santa Maria, "-- observed a light glimmering at a great distance. It vanished and reappeared several times during the night, moving up and down, in sudden and passing gleams. It was sighted 4 hours before land was sighted, and taken by Columbus as a sign they would soon come to land."*

1790, the French police saw them- *During the summer, Police Inspector Liabeuf witnessed and investigated a large red globe as it flew over farmland. The globe landed and a man came out and spoke in a language none understood. The globe then exploded and the man disappeared. The event was witnessed by many and is well documented.*

1897, a U.S. President saw them- *In a sworn statement, Alexander Hamilton said, "Last night about 10:30 we were awakened by a noise among the cattle. ---upon going to the door saw to my utter astonishment that an airship was slowly descending upon my cow lot, about 40 rods from the house". Then Hamilton also described it as a cigar shaped object, about 300 feet long with a carriage underneath. The carriage was of some transparent material. It was brightly lighted within. It contained six of the strangest beings he had ever seen.*

1915, a regiment of men may have been taken- *During World War I, a regiment of the British Army, the 1st 4th Norfolk, disappeared in an attempt to take Hill 60 near Gallipoli. In front of over 20 witnesses, the regiment, with over 800 men, marched into a strange formation of "lenticular clouds" that was hovering over Hill 60 and was never seen again. Posted as missing, the regiment was thought to have been captured. After the war, Britain demanded the return of the regiment, but the Turks denied any knowledge of the regiment's existence. No trace of the regiment has ever been found.* ***[The Turks could have been lying, but what do you do with 800 bodies?]***

241

Flying Pilots

There may be many answers to that question and I'm not getting into that at this time, instead we need to look at pilots. Some of the pilots of the strange flying vehicles seen recently have, evidently, been recovered from downed craft. They look extremely similar to the descriptions of the Dropa in ancient China that crash-landed about 12,000 years ago. Many scoff at the pictures saying they are Hollywood dummies, but if they are, what about those found thousands of years ago? The description of the Dropa indicated that they were big headed, small bodied humans that were delicate, fearful, and easily killed by the other inhabitants. Below are supposedly some of the not-so-fortunate pilots. Maybe their ancestors were the 'outer space Dropa" that wrote about their misfortunes on the 716 "twelve-thousand-year-old disk books" found in China that I discussed in book 3.

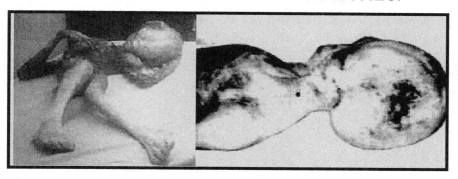

Why The Big Head?

OK! I just brought out this section without so much as a why the people look this way. Some had decided they look different than us so they must not be human. As I mentioned in the first book the probability that someone has been staying around the earth

243

watching us change and develop over the last million years is so improbable that it should not be used as a basis for theory without some pretty challenging absurdities being resolved. The pilots of the flying ships didn't come from another world. They came from Earth.

In book 3 I presented a theory that showed how the Seraphimic Nephilim bred with "normal" humans to form a different looking group of people. The seraphim themselves had reptilian characteristics and as they mated with "normal" humans, some of the traits began to come out in this somewhat strange group of humans whose depictions have been found around the world. The group of pilots described by witnesses today and depicted dozens of times during the fairly recent "ancient times" confirms a similarity to the Seraphimic hybrids.

That may have been the cause for reptilian skin and even the shoulder bumps, but many of the features don't make sense such as the huge eyes, oversized head, small nostrils and other features that are common to depictions of pilots seen today and those seen many years ago. The details of why the human pilots have a slightly different appearance will be a topic of discussion in book 8. The discussion involves "cows and the moon". Right now, let's just examine some of the evidence that there was a group of big headed, almond eyed, broad shouldered, possibly repltilianish, small nosed, HUMANS that were here and associated with flying ships.

Bad Artists

Some people may say that the reason the depictions below don't look like people is that the artists simply were no good, but other items found in these same locations prove that this is not the case. The people were excellent artists. The subjects were the strange ones. The creatures depicted probably looked very similar to the drawings and statuettes shown.

Pilots from Africa

Pilots from Egypt-Maybe their ancestors visited Egypt. Look at the drawing on the left found in Saqqara and see if is not the same type of individual Note the small mouth, wide almond shaped eyes, and almost non-existent nose. These were not normal inhabitants. This guy was depicted near something that looked like a rocket.

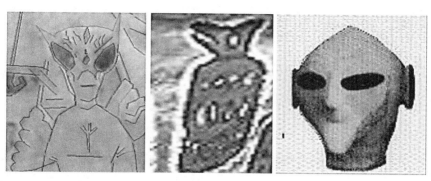

Pilots from Southern Africa-More strange visitors can be found in Africa. The depiction of the Dogan alien is the same as everywhere else in the ancient world. Note the large, slanted eyes, large head, strange suit, and apparent capability to float in the air or flying [no feet- above middle].

Pilots from North Africa-The characteristic facial features can be seen in this bust from the once major city in Tunis, Africa. Notice the smile these humans were a happy lot. [Above right]

Pilots from the South Seas

Easter Island-On the Island was found a stone head with an uncharacteristic beard, insect eyes, and two rays sprouting from head. Sounds like our other friends, doesn't it? There may be a connection of these creatures and the flying saucers seen today, but the main thing to remember here is that this type of "human" has been around for a long time. They probably even existed before the flood. Where they came from and where they are now is a mystery. I am not going to try to answer that particular question in this book. Book 8 may provide some clues to where they came from and what they are doing.

Australia-In *Australia,* we find this same creature. Large eyes, almost nonexistent nose. There is not much confusion with this being and "normal" humans. Could these have been ancestors of the pilots seen today? [Next left]

Pilots in New Zealand -We find the same being portrayed. The emblem is of the Hei-Tiki. A "<u>sky god</u>" identical to that made by the Sumerians half way across the globe. [Above Right]

Middle Eastern Pilots

This selection comes from the Sumerians, from the city of Jericho and from the Negev Desert.

Pilots from Sumeria-In Sumeria the apparent pilots had similar Alien features. Note the almond eyes, almost non-existent nose, small chin, and miniature mouth on their drawings and statues as shown in the 4 drawings below. The "people" were not from around here and the citizens shared with us their unusual characteristics. The 4 bumps on the shoulder or the first specimen are found on several images.

The Large almond shaped eyes and almost nonexistent nose give this humanoid away. He was not like the other inhabitants, but the commonness of the image should assure us that this was a real being living "or flying" in the area.

***Pilots from Jericho*-In** Jericho, 8-thousand-year-old depictions of strange humanoids could have been similar creatures. A couple *are shown below.*

Pilots from the Negev-In the Negev Desert of Israel, were found copper sheets with unusual drawings of alien-like people which have similarities to the others. Large eyes, non-existent nose. Drawings and actual pictures found are shown to the right. They appeared to be floating or flying on the drawing.

Far Eastern Pilots

This selection comes from all over the Far East including Pakistan, China, and Nepal. These representative pilots seem very similar to those seen in Africa, the Middle East, and in the South Pacific.

Pilots from Pakistan- In ancient Mohenjo-Daro not only do we find the exact same type of creature, but also it becomes evident that not only were they pilots of the flying ships, they also live among the "normal" people. Note again the almond eyes, miniature nose, broad shoulders, small chin, and large skulls. Note the 4 knobs on the shoulder and compare them to the first pilot pictured from Sumeria above. [Left image below]

Pilots from Nepal -In Nepal, still another indication of the strange visitors was found. A carved plate has been found which was manufactured around 4 thousand years ago. The carvings on the plate shows a large headed beings similar to that depicted today and an elliptical shaped object above him, which is very similar to reported UFOs of today. [Second Image above]

Japanese Pilots-Dozens of these "suited" statues have been recovered. Note the huge eyes, non-existent nose and unusual garment that looks extremely uncomfortable. What were these individuals trying to protect themselves from? Maybe they were trying to hide bumps on their shoulder. Or allow the wearer to breathe in outer space, assuming he was a pilot of a flying ship. [3rd Image]

Pilots from China-In China can be found many statuettes depicting humanoid creatures that are slightly odd. They have almond shaped eyes, which, by itself might not be strange in China, but almost no nose and small slit for a mouth, and reptilian like skin all point to another group that is no longer here. They almost looked like a cat in the face. Note the bump on the shoulder. Could it have been the Sumerian bumps? [Last image above]

More Chinese Pilots-If you remember from book 4, this is one of the Descendants of the Dropa, who settled in China some 12 thousand years ago. It is believed that his ancestors had been pilots as well.

Pilots from the Americas

In both South America and Central America, we find similar images. They aren't what you typically think of as human, but they have human characteristics just the same.

Utah Pilots-Note the broad shoulders, large eyes and almost nonexistent nose just like all the others. Also notice the bumps on the shoulders. These people were not drawn to look scary. This was most likely a close representation of what the artist had seen. Note how the one looks like he is floating. [Next left]

Pilots from Mexico-The identical types of people were seen in Mexico during post-flood, ancient times and pictorially represented to sustain the historical record. To the right are three of the many depictions of this creature found throughout Central and South America. Note the almond eyes, miniature nose, broad shoulders, small chin, and large skulls. Note the bumps depicted on both arms.

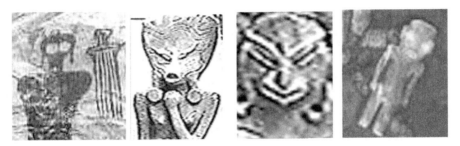

Pilots from Peru-Maybe their ancestors visited Peru. Look at these skulls found in South America. "Aliens" were everywhere in the early days. If the skull didn't come from a humanoid that was similar to the pilots found today, what did it come from? [First 2 images below]

Pilots from Chile-This giant drawing on the ground shows a similar pilot . Note the miniature nose [in fact no nose], broad shoulders, small chin, and bumps similar to the Sumerian depiction. In this case there are only 2 shown, but it is substantially different than today's humans. [Above third]

Pilots from Venezuela-This statuette of a baby was found at Lake Maracaibo. While the child had not developed the broad shoulders or the mysterious bumps, the facial features tell us she was somewhat different. [See last above]

Middle Aged UFOs

So far, we have seen testimony of sightings and pictures and carvings of not completely humanlike humanoids, but there is even more evidence that some strange flying was going on even through the Middle Ages. People didn't have cameras in those old days, but they may have had something almost as good. They had painters. Fantastic painters that saw UFOs just like many have done today. The collage below seems pretty much like what has been reported today as unidentified flying objects, but these portions of paintings came from the Middle Ages.

The image above shows 2 flying machines with people in them and flames coming out of the back. Some might think the painter was painting angels that had not yet learned how to fly on their own, or they were simply jokes played on the person who contracted the painting, but those possibilities would be wrong. People saw UFOs during the middle ages and painted them so others might experience them as well. They started showing up on many, many paintings, the following collage shows a small sampling of flying saucers depicted in middle ages paintings.

Three Orbed Feet, Portals,& Passengers-If we look at the two in the second column a little more closely, the details are remarkably similar to the flying objects reported today.

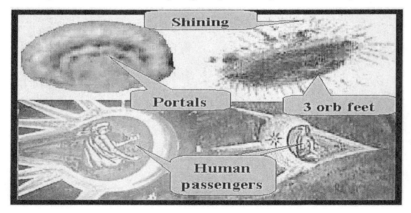

The two on the bottom are from the first painting shown. They clearly, show human passengers who were believed to have been in these strange ships. As shown below, many saw these "ships" so clearly, they could make out features including portals; glowing beams; and saucer shapes just like our present-day phenomenon.

During the Middle Ages people kept on seeing strange flying machines in the sky just like we do today, and as I showed, the pilots have been seen, are humanoid and somewhat similar to us.

The Next Book

Like I mentioned, from here we will need to travel to the 20th century to complete the investigation of the pilots of UFOs and that must be covered in another book.

Book 8 UFOs-Book 8 is not focused on the flying saucer phenomenon, but we will see more of these strange objects as witnessed in the 20th century. Then I will attempt to explain two important topics; just where these guys possibly came from recently and why they are here and have been here many times over the last few thousand years. I cannot convince myself that they came from outer space, but they must be from somewhere. Too many people have seen them for us to ignore their existence.

Book 8 Future-In addition to this explanation other elements of the 20th century will be dissected just as was done in the previous books. Finally, what lies in our future will be re-foretold by 2000-year-old writings, and 500-year-old seers. You will be amazed at the accuracy of the prophetic words of these ancient people. You should also be concerned about our near-term fate.

By the way, the earth probably is not going to go into some type of ozone depleted global warming cycle as you have been told. The earth is expected to have an Ice Age in the near future according to scientists and satellite data.

Once we know our present and future, book 8 will end the series and by most accounts the remaining people have a happy ending.

Conclusions

This book started just after the Greek Dark Ages and discussed the history of humans up until the 20th century.

1. By 900BC, the Jews had lost control of the Middle East.

2. All the Nephilim had been killed or died before the Jews lost control. You would think that men would get along without these taskmasters dreaming up wars, but they didn't.

3. Each small group of humans wanted to control another group of humans. There has been much written about this time period in man's history, so the book wasn't written so much as a continuous history, but instead was written as a history addendum. I only brought out areas I thought should have been expanded or revisited to broaden our vision of this time period. I tried to show that some information has been purposefully kept from most of us in an effort to keep everyone happy.

4. The focus of this book was on American history, but some other information was provided about other elements of human existence tracking around the world.

5. Hopefully I have shown that Columbus was not the first, nor the greatest, traveler to the Americas.

6. The Pilgrims were not the innocent people portrayed in our histories.

7. The one time period in American history that was not detailed was the Civil War. Detail accounting of battles and war

methodologies as well as the REAL reasons for the strife during that time period is identified in another book.

8. The fact that UFOs and the pilots of these strange flying vehicles were seen during the Middle Ages and before was examined on an initial level to show that they were and are real.

That being said, I did purposefully skew the discussion away from mainstream rather than presenting both sides. Generally, people know the other side. I brought out problems with our form of government, not because we have significant problems, because the American political element is more fair and better than that of almost all other countries. Unfortunately, if we blindly ignore what is happening around us, we could get into serious trouble.

The reason all of the uncomfortable information was brought out was to get you thinking.

About the Author

Steve Preston is a long lime author of scientific, esoteric facts. His books focus on the painful truths rather than whitewashed details that make us comfortable. If you are interested in the truth instead of comfort, please review other works by Mr. Preston as shown below. The images are some from Egypt on the left. To the right the writer is shown with his investigative friends in the Jewish Negev desert of Israel where the Dead Sea Scrolls were found that were used by John the Baptist in his Essene-like teachings.

Other investigations are also shown. To the left below are a couple of pictures as we searched the New Zealand caves possibly visited by the ancient Maori and the last image is of the author investigating the statues on the Acropolis in Athens Greece.

A list of most of my books are listed next. Besides this last group on time-travel, his books include a wide assortment of different subjects including Biblical History and proofs, the story of man's development, ancient tecnology, new views of physics and biology, ancient wars, current fears and events. A partial list follows:

Development of Mankind
The First Creation of Man-book 1 History of mankind
The Second Creation of Man-book 2 History of mankind
The Creation of Adam and Eve-book 3 History of mankind
The Antediluvian War Years-book 4 History of mankind
Man After The Flood-book 5 History of mankind
A Closer Look at Ancient History-book 6 History of mankind
A New View of Modern History-book 7 History of mankind
The Twentieth Century and Beyond- book 8 History of Mankind

Biblical History
Adam's First Wife-Story of Lilith
Incarnations of God- How often did God become Incarnated?
History Confirmed By The Bible- Science confirmation of the Bible
Moses Saved Egypt- How the Jews eliminated the Hyksos
Mysteries of the Exodus- Proofs of the Exodus
Why the King James Bible Failed- Issues with KJB

Bible Analysis
Abraham to Moses-First part of the Bible
Adam to Abraham- Second Part of the Bible
Moses to Jesus- Third part of the Bible Series
Understanding the New Testament-4th part of the Bible Series
Closer Look At Genesis- 200 ancient text confirm Genesis
Exploring Exodus- Reviewing the Details of "Exodus"
Errors in Understanding- Interpretations of the Bible
Expanded Genesis- Apocrypha and other Jewish texts
New look at the Bible- Questions in Interpretation
Old Testament Used By Jesus- Ancient Jewish texts
Exploring Genesis- Reviewing the details of "Genesis'

Ancient Technology and Life
Amazing Technology- Pleistocene Technology
Nephilimic Gods- History of the Ancient Giant/gods

Ancient History of Flying- Ancient flying
Kingdoms Before the Flood- Pleistocene humans
Living on Venus- Venus before the Pleistocene Extinction
Martians- Ancient Life on Mars
Mysterious Pyramids- Who made the Pyramids?
Victory of the Earth- History of our Earth
Not from Space- UFOs are not from space.
Space Anomalies-Anomalies and Analysis of space
Secrets of Thoth- Analysis of the 7 tablets of Thoth
Amazing Technology- Descriptions of prehistoric capabilities

Ancient and Modern War
America's Civil War Lie- Truth about the Civil War years
Behind the Tower of Babel- Story of the Bharata War
Driven Underground- Fear in the Bharata War
Four Armageddons- The 4 major wars that destroyed mankind
Six Deaths of Man- Destructions of mankind
World War Before- The Pleistocene War
World War with Heaven- The Angel and Nephilim War
World War Zero-The Bharata War
When Giants Ruled the Earth- History of the Titan Giants
Sex Crazed Angels- What caused the Heaven War?

Current Events and Fears
Allah' God of the Moon- Terror of Muslims
American School Disaster- fear in our country
Can We Save America? - Fear in the USA
Scythians Conquer Ireland- A History of Ireland
Fast History of MILES Training- Laser based Army training
Great American Quiz- Unusual details of American History
Make Your Own Global Warming-Tricks that look like warming
Modern Misconception- Misconceptions in Science
Truth About Phoenicia- The Evidence -First in America
Monsters are Alive- Post Pleistocene Monsters
Promote the General Welfare- Fear in USA
Our Very Odd Presidents- President review
Terror of Global Warming- Fake issue uncovered
The Antichrist- Many demonic possessed rulers

259

The Bad Side of Lincoln- Negative side of a great man
The Devil- Of Demons and their master
Vampires among Us- How Demons and Vampires are similar
Humans on Display- Slavery and Human Zoos
Romans Found America- American Trade before Columbus

New Look at Physics
Anthropic Reality- We control our Reality
Consensus Science- Fake Science
Complex Earth- Truth behind Earth's development
Is Time Travel Possible? Science of Time Travel
Retiming the Earth- Eliminate of Nuclear Decay Errors
Releasing Your Consciousness- Beyond our SELF
Slip Through a Wall- How to walk through solids
Our 12-Dimensional Universe- New science of our Universe
Mystery of Photons and Light- Science of Photons
Of Heaven and Hell- scientific descriptions
Meaning of Life and Light- Detains of New Science
Vibrational Matter- New Science of Quantum Fluctuations
Incredible Tesla- Examination of his discoveries
Death Without Death-The Life of one's Soul

New Look at Biology
Understand Your Heart- New discoveries of the Heart Brain
DNA of Our Ancestors- Tracing DNA of ancient man
God Didn't Make The Ape- New science on ape Evolution
Lizard People- Mutated People of the Bharata War
Creation and Death of Dinosaurs- Why Dinosaurs died
Races of Men- Tracing DNA of Humans
Tracing Cro-Magnon to Jesus- The third creation and mutation
Self, Soul, Spirit- Three components of Life
Self-Virtualization- New science of reality
True Happiness- Self Actualism and Beyond
Life Resonance- Unusual capabilities of men
Awaken the Departed- We can talk to the Dead
Biophotonics and Healing- How Photonics used in medicine

Time Traveling Empath Historical Fiction

Conrad and the Flood- James aids survivors of the Pleistocene Extinction

Shama and the Tower- James aids the survival of India during the Aryan Invasion

Naille and the Exodus- James aids the survival of Jews & Scythians of the Exodus

Secrets of Washington- James insures Washington become President